LIVING WITH LOSS

FACING GRIEF AND ADVERSITY IN A SOCIETY THAT DOESN'T UNDERSTAND

CORTEZ RANIERI

CONTENTS

This book is dedicated to anyone facing the struggle of loss. You're not alone on this journey. It's time to challenge the status quo and create a better life.

INTRODUCTION

"It is better to conquer our grief than to deceive it. For if it has withdrawn, being merely beguiled by pleasures and preoccupations, it starts up again and from its very respite gains force to savage us. But the grief that has been conquered by reason is calmed forever. I am not therefore going to prescribe you those remedies which I know many people have used, that you divert or cheer yourself by a long or pleasant journey abroad, or spend a lot of time carefully going through your accounts and administering your estate, or constantly be involved in some new activity. All those things help only for a short time; they do not cure grief but hinder it. But I would rather end it than distract it."

— SENECA

As a young boy just entering my teen years, I lost my mother to a devastating battle with cancer. One day, she was raising me and giving me a great childhood. The next, I watched her deteriorate as she battled to the best of her ability. After she passed, the weight of her absence hit me like a freight train, and the grieving process quickly followed.

Through my adolescence and into my adult years, I realized that healing is not entirely linear. I would have moments of pure sadness, followed by feelings of rage or anger. On the days that I felt okay, I almost thought that I wasn't supposed to be happy. Above all, I was confused by what I was feeling and how long it lasted. I just wanted my mom back, and I wanted life to feel normal again.

After the loss of my mother, I was left feeling isolated from society. I allowed my sadness to rest deep inside my core, which caused me to become reclusive. There were times when I would not leave my house for days on end, even when my friends or family encouraged me to spend time with them. I felt all alone, though I knew that I had support within reach.

If you have picked up this book, you are probably feeling some of what I have felt. No matter who you are grieving or how long it has been, the loss of a loved one is arguably the most impactful life event you will experience. At times, the grief becomes unbearable to the point that it seems you cannot go on any longer. A life without your loved one is impossible to imagine.

This overwhelming sadness tricks you into thinking that this is your new normal and that happiness will never be achieved again. But this is not the case. Grief comes in stages, and it won't overwhelm you forever. Because each stage lasts for various lengths of time, you cannot predict an exact end date to your suffering, but you can feel confident in knowing that the next stage is coming. You will be able to get through it and heal.

Unfortunately, grief does not only appear in mental suffering. It causes physical symptoms that wear you down as well. The result is a powerful force that should not be underestimated or ignored.

But that doesn't mean you have to let it control your life. In this book, you will learn all of the tools you need to successfully acknowledge and process the grief you are experiencing. Even on the days when you feel that you are too overwhelmed with your emotions, you will figure out how to work through them by using the tips and methods in this book. You will also learn how to surround yourself with the best people in your life and find out ways to uplift yourself when you need an extra boost. This support will be vital to your healing.

Working through grief is a process. It is not something you should expect to handle overnight. Throughout your journey, you can expect to understand grief and how you can face the accompanying emotions, which is often one of the most difficult parts of healing. You will also learn:

- The physical and emotional symptoms of grief
- How to differentiate between grief and depression
- A detailed guide on the five steps of grief
- How to find solace in Stoicism
- How to face your pain directly

- How to deal with feelings of anger and rage
- The Wim Hof Method of dealing with grief

By the time you are through reading, you will feel like a weight has been lifted from you. You will have the ability to work through your feelings until you reach a point where you can celebrate the memory of your loved one who has passed.

I wrote this book because I understood that the way I felt when I lost my mother as a young boy is the way that a lot of people feel on a regular basis. Through years of research, I have come to understand the best ways to deal with loss. I hope for this book to guide you through all of the stages of grief as they come to you, and I believe that my research on the topic will assist you through them.

I have written another book titled *10 Habits for Grief and Loss: Create Change Through Adversity to Become a Better You* that details an abundance of healthy habits you can implement in your life to guide you through your grieving period. The goal of both books is to make you stronger both physically and emotionally. I am passionate about helping people, and I want to help you return to the person you once were before the grief entered your life.

By acknowledging your pain now instead of pushing it aside, you are one step closer toward acceptance and living a better life.

1

KNOW YOUR ENEMY

G rief is a powerful force to be reckoned with, yet you cannot see it in a tangible form. It weaves its way through you, getting tangled up in your emotions and thoughts. Most everyone will experience this pain at some point, but each individual will have a unique way of dealing with and processing grief. Some may begin the process right away, sorting through their anger, denial, and uncertainty. Others will need time to get there, often spending time mourning the loss until they reach a depressive state. Your version of grieving is not incorrect or wrong. You are feeling the loss, so you get to decide what you are going to do to mourn it.

The most important thing is to take care of yourself as you feel all of this intensity. Many people completely shut down after experiencing a loss because they feel it is too painful to go on. If you ever start to feel this way, stop for a moment to assess your situation. There are certain parameters that you can learn to better guide you on your path. Grief might not always look identical, but there are plenty of recognizable contributing factors that you can become aware of. By having this knowledge, you will be able to help yourself through even the most difficult times.

Remember that grief is completely natural, and you need to experience it before you can heal from the loss. Grief asks you to open up your mind, body, and soul to the fact that the person you love is now gone. It can be difficult to feel these things, especially when you are forced into the grieving process before you can fully comprehend what you are feeling. Take your time with it. If you try to rush, you aren't going to properly experience all of the emotions required to heal.

Grief can make you feel numb, causing you to withdraw from life and the things you normally love to do. Even simple tasks like going to the grocery store can feel too difficult or painful while you are grieving. Because it can be easy to deteriorate when you are not taking care of yourself, having a solid support system is crucial. You need to have some people who you are willing to let in as you sort through your emotions. This is a personal experience, so there should be no shame in asking for help during this time.

When you are working through the grieving process, it is best to fully let go of the idea that you are going to control it. There is no controlling mourning, and you end up being able to sort through it better when you stop trying. Instead, your focus should be on picking yourself back up and thinking about the things that will make you feel better.

Before you can get to that point, though, you need to understand what you are dealing with, which means understanding how grief works. In general, there are five stages of grief, which include the following:

- Denial
- Anger
- Bargaining
- Depression
- Acceptance

You might experience them in that exact order, or you might only feel one stage for a long time until you are ready to move forward. Do not pressure yourself into believing that you need to be further ahead than you are. By listening to your heart, you can figure out how long you must stay at each stage, even if they come out of order.

Grief is accompanied by mourning. Mourning can last for an undetermined amount of time. You might be processing the loss for weeks, months, or even years. All of these options are valid because you are going through something personal. Take as much time as you need to work through a difficult time. Make sure you surround yourself with all of the best resources to help you. If you ever feel uncertain about your process and if it is becoming detrimental to your life or well-being, you can always consult a medical professional for more guidance.

MYTHS ABOUT GRIEVING AND LOSS

To better understand the process of grieving a loss, it helps to recognize some of the most common myths. Through this knowledge, you will be able to validate your experience and get through it successfully.

Myth: Grief and mourning are the same.

You can think of your grief as a storage space for all of the thoughts and feelings that you have surrounding the loss of your loved one. Picture your grief like a big box that can be filled with all of the memories, photographs, experiences, and feelings that you had with this person. Some days, it can feel good to look back at all of the mementos you have collected along the way. On other days, thinking about your loved one can feel incredibly difficult. These feelings are intense because grief typically activates quickly once you discover you have lost a loved one. Your grief gives the loss an internal meaning that you will likely hold on to until you feel secure enough to move forward in your healing process.

While grief is made up of your internal feelings, mourning is the outward expression of those feelings. Mourning occurs when you decide to do something with the grief that you are holding on to. This means that you are ready to take your internal thoughts and feelings and express them in an outward fashion. This may include crying, which is a sign that you have begun mourning.

Other methods of mourning may include journaling, creating artwork based on the individual, talking about good memories you had with them, praying, and celebrating special dates that are relevant to that individual. Choose whichever one feels right to you.

To heal, you must reach the point of mourning because grieving is only going to keep your difficult feelings inside of you.

Myth: Women grieve more than men.

This notion likely stems from the idea that women tend to be more open and in touch with their emotions. In society, men are typically scolded or made fun of when they cry or express strong emotions. Therefore, it is thought that men are more hesitant to cry and get in touch with their grief because of these social constructs that have been in place for a long time.

In reality, grief does not discriminate, and both women and men can experience varying intensities when it comes to grief. Everybody deserves a chance to grieve properly regardless of gender identity. If you are a man who is going through the grieving process, remember that your feelings do not make you weak. Loss is a difficult subject to accept, and you need to do your best to reach this point.

To stop perpetuating this myth, it is necessary to support those who are grieving. Their experience might not make sense to you, just as yours might not make sense to others, but the support is going to make a big difference.

Myth: Not thinking about your pain will make it disappear.

This might work for a little while, but it is not a permanent solution. Instead, it leads to a stage called denial. Typically, this stage happens at the beginning of your grief, but it can enter again at any point.

When you live in denial, things might feel bearable. You stop thinking about your pain, so you stop feeling uncomfortable. Living in an ignorant state of mind makes it seem like you are healing without having to deal with the painful parts. What is often overlooked is the fact that this only suppresses emotions.

Eventually, they are going to come up again, often when you least expect them. And this time, they will be stronger because stifling your emotions makes them even more intense. While everything might feel okay on the surface, it only takes a small trigger to bring them back into the foreground of your life.

Although it is hard, it is best to experience your raw pain as soon as you can to fully process it. This is how you are going to make important steps toward being fully healed from the loss.

Myth: The first year is the hardest.

You will often hear people say that the first year after you lose someone is the hardest you have to experience. This puts the idea in your head that the years to follow are going to be easier. While the first year does have a particularly difficult feeling because you are going to be cycling through all of the holidays and special times of the year without this person, it does not necessarily become easier the next year. It might, or it might feel even more difficult because you are aware of all of the time that has passed.

You might experience several great years of making progress with the loss, only to feel derailed and back where you started in the first year. This is a normal part of the process, which is why it is so individual. You never know what you are going to experience, but going with the flow is going to allow you to navigate through it all. Do not put any pressure on yourself by falsely promising that the first year will be the worst. You do not know what might happen in the future, but this does not mean you should live fearfully. Take care of yourself as time goes on, and you will learn how to handle anything that comes your way.

Myth: Grief is a single emotion.

When you think about grief, you likely imagine sadness and tears. These can be big aspects of the grieving process, but they are not the only ones. Grief can take on many different appearances, some of which may surprise you.

Grief can come through as intense anger or rage, both for the situation and at the person lost. It can feel like confusion and being lost in a haze. You might also find yourself gravitating toward things that make you laugh or that make you happy because this is a defense mechanism against sadness.

No matter what you are feeling during your grieving process, be mindful of it. Never shame yourself for the way you feel because you cannot help this, just as you could not help that you lost someone you cared about. If you start to act out of character, understand that it might be the grief trying to get your attention. This can be an indication that you might be ready to start the mourning process and release your grief in an outward expression.

Myth: Grief is bad.

While grief *feels* bad, it is not inherently bad. You are going to have to process many difficult thoughts and feelings during this process, but the process itself is a positive one. Remind yourself that you have to work through these hard times to get to the point of happiness again. Only through recognizing your grief will you be able to find the path toward healing. If anyone tries to make you feel bad for the way you are grieving or the length of time you are grieving, they are not someone you need to keep close to you during this time.

Normalize grief because it is entirely natural. If you feel any kind of guilt or bad feelings about the way you are grieving, be easy on yourself. You are not doing anything wrong by exploring these feelings and trying to get to the bottom of them. You do not deserve to live with their burdens forever. It is brave to take an actionable step forward during your grieving process. Be proud of yourself for trying, even when you do not succeed right away.

Myth: There's a right way to grieve.

There is no standard or any rules when it comes to the way you experience grief. If anyone tries to tell you that you are doing it wrong or if you begin to second-guess yourself, remind yourself that it is an individualized experience. Only you know what it feels like to lose the loved one you did. Only you have the memories that you have with them, and you shared all of the experiences that you did. Your grief is not going to look the same as the grief of others, even if it is based on the loss of the same person. Human connections are so diverse, and only you know exactly what it felt like to be connected to the person you lost.

You will find a way that feels right for you, but this does not mean it is the only way. Since there are no rules in place, you get to try several different methods until you start to feel better. There is a lot of room for self-exploration in the process of grieving. You can take advantage of this by being willing to try different methods until you start to feel better. It might be incredibly difficult to take the leap, but it will prove to be worthwhile over time.

Myth: You can only grieve a death.

This is an interesting concept to explore. When people express that they are grieving, you probably jump to the conclusion that they have experienced a death. But grief can appear even when death is not involved. Losing something important to you can trigger symptoms of grief in the same way. The loss of a job is one example. If you get fired or laid off from the job that provided you with a stable income, you are placed in a position of loss that likely makes you feel uncertain. You might even feel like you are in denial in the beginning, and the anger will follow.

Losing a friendship due to betrayal is another instance when you might feel the need to grieve. Maybe a trusted person has proven to be untrustworthy, which is a jarring discovery to accept. You might become depressed from the devastation, and you will have to reach a point of acceptance before you feel okay about it. This is similar to the way you must move forward when you are grieving the death of a loved one.

Myth: Children do not grieve and should not attend funerals.

Much like any other individual, children can feel loss and grief in big ways. Their process might look different depending on how old they are and how well they can grasp the concept of death, but it is still grief. Allowing children the chance to express themselves during grief is so important. When they are not given any outlets for their grief, they can begin to internalize all of the anger and confusion, which can turn into detrimental mental health issues in the future.

Regarding funerals, this is a personal decision. A lot of children can grasp the concept of loss, and in some cases, a funeral might provide them with the necessary closure to help them make sense of the loss endured. This all depends on the child and how they are coping, but it is a good idea to observe their behaviors to determine if attending a funeral might put them at ease.

These are among the most common myths that circulate regarding grief. You have probably heard some of them before, and maybe you even believe them yourself. Now that you are learning more about the process, you can open your mind to new ideas surrounding grief and how to get through it.

PHYSICAL SYMPTOMS

When you are going through grief, you feel emotionally depleted. While this impacts your mind, it also impacts your body.

People going through grief often describe it as a debilitating illness. Not feeling your best physically tends to bring down your mood. Your body is also less capable of warding off illnesses because your immune system suffers. You need a certain amount of energy to function properly, and your grief can deplete this entirely.

Consider a study published in the journal *Ageing and Immunity*, which discovered that elderly people who have experienced the recent loss of a loved one were more at risk of developing infectious diseases (Romm 2014). When you are in so much emotional distress, you feel the heartbreak quite literally. This is why staying deep within your grief can be dangerous. Your body becomes weakened, susceptible to illness.

The last thing that you want to experience while you are mourning the loss of a loved one is the decline of your health. It is no secret that the older you get, the harder it is for your body to fight against potential illnesses. But what happens when age is combined with grief?

A study administered by the University of Birmingham's School of Sport observed two groups of mourners. One group had an average age of 32, while the other had an average age of 72. They used similarly aged control groups of individuals who had not experienced a recent loss. Throughout the study, the older mourners were found to have a weakened function in their neutrophils, which are the white blood cells found in the body that help fight against infections. While the younger group of mourners saw plenty of similar psychological symptoms, they didn't see the same physiological symptoms. Therefore, the study confirmed that those who are older are more biologically at risk of becoming ill after experiencing a loss (Romm 2014).

A further explanation of the above study states that there is a bigger difference between the older group of mourners and the younger group because of the stress hormone known as cortisol. By the time an individual reaches the age of 30, a person's DHEA levels drop. This is the hormone that typically balances your cortisol levels. With lower DHEA levels the older you get, the weaker your immune system becomes. Any exposure to prolonged depression or sadness due to a loss can become detrimental the older you are.

Aside from weakening your immune system, grief can take over other systems in your body that keep you healthy and functioning properly. When you are experiencing grief, you experience an increase in inflammation. In general, inflammation in any part of your body can become negative because it can worsen existing health problems and lead to new ones. When your body is constantly trying to fight against inflammation, its response system can start damaging healthy cells because it is being overworked. This is why you might experience different health problems that you've never had before.

The condition of your heart health is also worsened when you are experiencing grief. This is especially true if you are stuck in a cycle of grief for a prolonged time. Because of this, you are more prone to heart disease and high blood pressure. Some intense grief can even lead to a syndrome known as broken heart syndrome. This is a form of heart disease that appears similar to a heart attack, further proving how powerful the sadness of grief can become if not addressed properly. This is a scary ailment to experience because it can happen suddenly.

Through all of the physical distress, you are also more prone to develop panic attacks. Even though panic attacks usually occur due to mental triggers, they cause physical responses. Often, a panic attack includes increased heart rate, trembling/shaking, chills or hot flashes, tightness in your chest, and sweating. The panic takes over and convinces you that there is lingering doom ahead with nothing you can do to stop it.

The Common Link

As you navigate through your grief, the physical and emotional symptoms are connected by the stress you feel. When you are under a lot of stress, the systems in your body that control your physical and emotional stress are bound to overlap. As you are feeling more stressed out, your body is receiving signals to activate certain protective processes in your nervous system. In other words, your mind and body are working harder than ever. This is why it is easy to get sick when you are going through the process of mourning. Your stress can become chronic if left untreated, and this will cause you to rapidly deteriorate.

Many people are ashamed of the physical symptoms they feel because they do not want to appear weak or a burden. Remember that it is completely normal to be physically impacted by your grief. This does not make you an inconvenience to be around or a selfish person. Loss is difficult to comprehend and to address, so the way that you respond to it is often outside of your control. As you begin to move through the stages, you will learn how to process each symptom and take care of yourself again.

You may need reminders to practice self-care. When you are grieving the loss of a loved one, you are the last person that you are thinking about. All of the memories that you have with this person are likely occupying the space in your brain, and you often have little room to think about anything else. It can become easy to forget how to make yourself feel better or to even complete basic tasks, such as eating, sleeping, and showering. Before you get to this point of physical neglect, you must address all of the thoughts and feelings that you are having without judgment. You have every right to remember your loved one and to miss them, but you must remind yourself to stay on a safe path and to continue to take care of yourself in the process.

To keep yourself in check, consider the following physical symptoms of grief. If you notice them happening to you, they can serve as a sign to slow down and to take better care of yourself:

- Stomach pain
- Fatigue
- Chest tightness
- Decreased appetite
- Nausea
- Shortness of breath
- Dry mouth
- Headache

- Sweating

While these are not all of the physical symptoms you can experience, they are among the most common. Only you know how you are feeling physically, so you must pay close attention to these symptoms. If you feel that they are getting worse, it might be necessary to contact a medical professional for help. There is no shame in getting help during the process of mourning because it is a difficult one. Not everybody can navigate through it alone, and that is nothing to be ashamed of.

Remember that your biological makeup can also be an influential factor in this process. If you are older or already have physical ailments that you struggle with, then you are more susceptible to the physical symptoms of grief.

If you realize that you are experiencing these symptoms but do not require professional help, tune into them. Notice how your body feels and acknowledge why. This becomes an extension of your acceptance of the loss. Once you can identify your physical symptoms and understand that they are happening to you because of the grief, you can make a plan to heal from them and finally move forward in your process. Much like the emotional factors of grief, the physical factors also do not have a set timeline. You might feel bad for a few weeks, months, or years. It all depends on how your body processes the experience.

EMOTIONAL AND BEHAVIORAL CHANGES

If you feel that you haven't been yourself since the grief began, it is likely that your emotions and behaviors have been changing, which is common. While the process is different for each person, losing a loved one can trigger certain changes within that you might not recognize at first.

It can be alarming to one day notice that you are acting differently. You might also feel defensive when others in your life point out these changes. The best way to handle them if they start happening to you is to remain aware of them. By noticing any changes that you experience, you will have a better idea of what you need to do to heal from the grief and how to get through it in a healthy way. The below symptoms are explained to give you an idea of what you might be going through.

Anxiety

Anxiety can change a lot about your behavior. It can lead you to believe that something bad is going to happen to other loved ones in your life and maybe even cause you to question your mortality. When you experience anxiety, you have a worrying feeling that you cannot seem to shake. You might not be able to identify what exactly you are worried about, but the feeling can become persistent. There are plenty of instances that can trigger your anxiety that extend beyond thinking about the death of your loved one, which is why it can be tricky to realize that it is the cause.

Your anxiety triggers are personal, and they are valid. For example, if your loved one died in a car accident, you might find yourself triggered by something like the slamming of a car door.

You cannot help what triggers you, but you can get help with your anxiety. Focusing on your breathing and practicing meditation can become beneficial to you during this time. For any additional help, there is the option of speaking with a mental healthcare professional.

Detachment

This symptom is particularly common in the beginning stages of grief. Right after you lose your loved one, you are probably going to experience some degree of denial. Because of this, you will find it hard to stay in touch with the reality of your life. Everything is bound to feel distant and difficult to comprehend, even if it is an entirely normal part of your routine. For example, you might not experience the same enjoyment from spending time with people you care about or watching your favorite television show because your mind is elsewhere.

While it is not a good feeling to realize that you are detaching from your life, it usually fades over time. As you begin to heal from the loss, you will slowly start to feel joy and happiness again that you thought you lost permanently.

The thing to remember about grief is that no stage is permanent. While it can feel that this is going to be forever, understand that it will pass. Your brain needs time to comprehend what has happened and to find paths that you can take to work your way through it. Be patient and gentle with yourself if you find that you are now detached.

Loneliness

After losing someone you truly care about, the feeling of loneliness can set in. Even if you have a great support system around you, these individuals are not the person that you lost. It is okay if you feel that their presence is not the same because it should not feel the same. Acknowledge the uniqueness and special qualities of the individual you are grieving. This appreciation for them can bring forth positive memories that you can hold on to. While you are going through this process, be sure to acknowledge when other people in your life want to be there for you.

Even if you are not ready to be around people yet, you still likely have plenty who care about you in your life. They want you to be okay and want to support you through this difficult period. Grief can present the illusion that you are all alone or that you are the only one who feels this way, but it is not true. If you feel that you cannot talk to anyone in your life about what you are going through, consider meeting with a grief counseling support group. This will put you in contact with others who are experiencing the loss of loved ones. Knowing that others can relate to you in similar ways will help the feeling of loneliness dissolve.

Lack of Concentration

When you experience a loss, it often takes over every thought. You might be going over the situation constantly in your mind, leaving you unable to focus on anything else. It is not uncommon to have difficulty working or keeping up with your responsibilities during this time. Being preoccupied with the situation does not feel good, and it keeps your mood low because you are constantly reminded of the loss.

Finding healthy distractions will help you accept that it is okay to think about other things. You might feel that you do not deserve to feel happy during this time, but this is only a temporary feeling, much like the other symptoms that come with grief. You can read an uplifting book or surround yourself with people who have positive energy. Getting out of your head and out of the thoughts that plague you will help you refocus your concentration.

Sleep Disturbances

When you are emotionally distressed, your sleep is prone to interruptions. This can manifest in different ways, including insomnia. You might feel unable to sleep or too worried to fall asleep. This can happen because you are constantly thinking about the person you lost or the fact that they are gone. If you have been tossing and turning all night long, you are not going to feel rested in the morning.

If you can get to sleep, you might end up waking up a lot. With this kind of interruption, you are not getting the deep sleep that you require to feel rested. Being unable to reach your REM sleep might make you feel like you haven't slept at all.

There is also the possibility that you will experience an increase in nightmares that wake you up. The thoughts that you have before you fall asleep or the thoughts that are in your subconscious can impact what you dream about. Talking about your feelings will help you let go of these thoughts. With a clear mind, you will be able to finally rest again.

Troubling Thoughts

The thoughts you have while you are grieving might scare you or worry you. Because you are so focused on the loss of your loved one, you might experience thoughts that you never used to have before. Some people end up thinking about death a lot more or their health. This can become overwhelming if these troubling thoughts do not leave your head, and they can also contribute to any sleep disturbances that you might be having. When you are left to overthink situations, you are much more likely to hold on to these thoughts and let them bother you.

If you want relief from them, you can journal or talk to someone you trust. You might not feel comfortable expressing all of your deepest thoughts to someone in your life, even if you do trust them, but journaling can serve as a good outlet for you during this time. The best thing about journaling is that nobody has to ever read it. You can say anything that you want in an uncensored way to get all of your thoughts off your mind. Imagine them staying on the page as you write them down, clearing up space in your head for some peace of mind.

Restlessness

This is a common coping mechanism that tends to develop during grief. If you feel that you cannot sit still, you might be fighting avoidance. This stems from the denial stage of grief, and it can change your behavior in a powerful way without you realizing it. Immersing yourself in activities that take up a lot of time or energy might be a way for you to cope with the loss. There is a fine line between a healthy level of activity and doing so much that you are simply avoiding the situation at hand. If you constantly feel restless, this can be a sign that you need to slow down and address your feelings rather than keeping yourself busy.

Let yourself feel okay with remaining still for a few moments a day, even if this is when the upsetting thoughts come up. This might be necessary for you to successfully move toward your next stage of grief. It is going to feel uncomfortable, but this is how you are going to make improvements in your life. You can work through this process slowly, only allowing a little bit in at a time. There is no need to burden yourself by being consumed with these thoughts, but there must be a balance between distraction and stillness.

Loss of Appetite or Comfort Eating

Your gut health is directly connected to your mental health. When you feel nervous or stressed out, this can stimulate your appetite in different ways. Some people eat comfort foods when they feel uncomfortable. The food serves as temporary relief to the problem they are experiencing. But letting yourself indulge every day can become an unhealthy coping mechanism. The food that you eat becomes the fuel that gets you through each day. If you are consuming a lot of processed foods, fried foods, artificial ingredients, or sugar, then you are putting yourself at risk of developing physical ailments. It is okay to treat yourself to the things that you love once in a while, but make sure you are doing so to enjoy them, not to mask your feelings.

On the opposite end of the spectrum, you might experience an entire loss of appetite. Depression or sadness can usually trigger this symptom of behavior. You might feel that you are too upset to perform basic actions. This can include the act of caring for yourself by feeding yourself. With all of the sadness that you feel, you might not want to think about food during this time.

Understand that you need to keep yourself healthy if you want to make a full recovery, and eating during this time is essential. Do your best to make sure you are eating meals regularly, even if the portions are smaller. When you eat less but eat more nutritious food, you will get enough vitamins and minerals to keep yourself physically healthy.

If you have been experiencing any of the above changes, do not allow this to scare you or worry you. While you should get help if you feel overwhelmed by them, you can feel hopeful that you are moving through a normal cycle of grief. These changes indicate that your mind and body are both aware that you are going through something painful and difficult. What they are trying to achieve is adaptation.

2

THE THIN LINE BETWEEN GRIEF AND DEPRESSION

M any believe that grief and depression are the same. While you are mourning the loss of a loved one, you are going to be put into a state of severe sadness, which can often manifest into depression. The two do not always go hand in hand, however. In this chapter, you will learn the key differences between the typical cycles of grief and the indicators of depression.

Because depression can appear suddenly and bring an onslaught of dangerous side effects, it is important to recognize when it is happening. Depression often takes over in such a powerful way that you do not even realize you are in it. By knowing what to look for, you can ensure that you are taking all of the right precautionary measures to have the safest grieving period that you can.

Since both display similar symptoms, it can often be confusing to tell the difference between grief and depression. Another factor that makes each one difficult to differentiate is that they often overlap. When the two are so intertwined, it can be hard to see where one starts and one ends. Commonly, periods of extended grief will lead to depression. While this is not always the case, this seems to be one of the most common triggers for depression. The following similarities and differences will help you see what you should be looking for.

THE SIMILARITIES

As you read through each of these similarities, you will see that they can all define grief and depression in certain ways. By navigating through each one, determining the emotions that you feel and where they stem from, and gauging how long you have been experiencing them, you will be able to better understand if you are going through a typical cycle of grief or if you have developed depression. If it turns out that you are depressed, the outlook is not hopeless. You still have a chance to work through your grief in a healthy way.

Sadness

You are probably already pretty familiar with sadness. As you experience various events in your life, even those unrelated to loss or death, you will feel sadness. From the earliest instances of your childhood, you were taught what it meant to be sad, perhaps when your parents told you that you could not spend time with your friends or that you could not get that toy at the store that you had been eyeing.

As we age, we feel sadness for reasons that evolve. Through adolescence, you will likely move away from caring so much about material possessions or decisions that your parents make for you and, instead, shift your focus to your social circle and romantic interests. This is the next stage developmentally, and most of us can say that we experienced a heartbreak or two during those emotionally charged years. With all of the hormones circulating through our bodies, it is almost impossible to feel happy all of the time.

Then, as an adult, sadness usually dissipates. You learn how to deal with the fact that you cannot always get what you want and that things do not always work out as planned. While there is plenty that still can make you feel sad, you usually develop coping mechanisms to help you through the feeling. There are different ways you can do this, both unhealthy and healthy. Some examples of healthy coping mechanisms include venting to loved ones, journaling your feelings, and seeking therapy.

When your sadness is out of your control, unhealthy coping mechanisms tend to appear. You might try to fill the void with material items or dangerous behaviors that are out of character. Instant gratification becomes prominent during this stage because you simply want to feel happy again. Sadness is powerful, but what most do not realize is that it does not have to be overpowering.

How this relates to grief and depression is fairly straightforward. It lasts for a long time, and there is little that you can do to change the way you feel. In cases of sadness that are brought on by grief, this is a stage that you go through. While it can last for an extended period, you can find your way to the next stage. The sadness does not take over your entire life, and you can find outlets to express yourself during this time.

When your sadness comes from depression, getting through it feels a lot harder. Because you are so discouraged about getting past it, you remain in your depressive state. Then, the other symptoms start appearing. All of the things you used to love that brought you happiness no longer feel the same. It becomes impossible to simply "snap out" of your sadness because it is a lingering feeling that can often feel daunting, and it typically requires extra help to work through.

No matter where your sadness is stemming from, there is no need to feel ashamed because of what you are feeling. We all experience pain differently, and emotional pain is no exception. Be gentle with yourself as you try to work through all of your feelings that surround the passing of your loved one. This is necessary before you can move past your sadness. You must experience it, even if it is difficult.

Insomnia

A symptom that affects your sleep, insomnia might not seem like a big deal at first. It is common to become restless or even fearful at night because this is when your brain tends to focus on what is bothering you. As you begin to unwind each day, your mind will likely review all of the things that are on it. This is problematic when you have suffered a loss because grief can bring forward a lot of painful and surprising emotions that you might not be aware of that are lurking below the surface.

Experiencing the loss of a loved one can be triggering for many reasons. If you have lost someone in the past, this new loss might trigger the same feelings that you went through before. Since you remember how terrible it was to grieve that individual, your brain might put up certain barriers to not have to go through the same process again, even though you need to do this. It becomes easy to mentally block out certain memories and thoughts when your brain is trying to protect you from feeling pain.

You might become triggered because you start to feel fearful that you are going to lose other people in your life who you care about. This can even manifest into a fear of losing other important things, such as your job, house, or car. Anything important to you can get taken away, and this is not a comfortable thought to focus on when you are going through grief.

If you find yourself unable to sleep at night, you are probably experiencing insomnia because of one of the above reasons. Your mind starts racing, the fear kicks in, and you begin replaying all of the thoughts that make you feel sad, uncomfortable, or scared. Your brain just wants to keep this from happening, so it remains in a hyperactive state that prevents you from fully resting. This can go on for hours or even entire nights.

Without proper sleep, you are going to feel the impacts in your daily life. It is a lot harder to complete your responsibilities at work and home when you haven't slept at night. Your interactions with other people also become strained because you are more likely to be in a bad mood. Sleep is how you function successfully, and without it, you are going to start acting differently.

It is normal to experience insomnia for a short amount of time when you are going through the loss of a loved one. This is likely to happen during the beginning of your process, and it will usually taper off as you begin to heal from the loss. If it persists for an extended time, this can be an indication that it is happening due to depression. The feeling is usually chronic when you are depressed and unable to sleep. It can also feel more intense.

Make sure that you are taking inventory of your mental health closely. If you notice that your lack of sleep is debilitating, then there is likely a need for intervention. There are many ways that you can guide yourself through this symptom, even if you do not seek therapy. By doing something relaxing before bed, such as yoga, reading a book, or drinking hot tea, you can put your mind at ease to the best of your ability. There are also natural remedies that you can take, like Melatonin, that promote that sleepy chemical in your brain.

Poor Appetite

One of the first signs of grief and depression you will notice is your lack of appetite. With both, the feeling hits you instantly because you will start refusing meals that you normally eat. What you eat to fuel your body is important normally, but this is especially true when you are going through a loss. The vitamins and nutrients you get from fueling your body with healthy foods make you feel physically stronger. Without them, you are going to deteriorate a lot faster.

Even if you are still eating, changing the portion size suddenly is still going to impact you because your body is used to eating a certain amount each day. This can lead to feelings of lethargy, laziness, or dizziness. The longer you experience this symptom, the more dangerous it can become. There are even some instances where your lack of appetite can trigger eating disorders, which seem like they will help you because you can be in control of what you are or are not putting into your body.

Be easy on yourself when you first notice that your appetite is not the same. You are processing a lot of new information and adjusting to life without a person who was important to you. Even when you do not feel like eating, try to encourage yourself to have meals that are small and packed with protein. While you might not be eating as much as you used to, having these smaller portions is better than not having anything at all.

With grief, this symptom should subside fairly quickly. You will feel it dissolve, much like insomnia, over time.

If you notice that it is not going away and that you are not eating at all, then this might be an indication that you are struggling with a bigger problem due to depression. Since depression can be chronic, so can your lack of appetite. You might find yourself going for several hours or even days without food. This is going to impact you both physically and mentally. When you are not refueling your body regularly, you are going to be running off of the little energy you have from sleeping.

Thinking about this one step further, if you are not sleeping, there is not much fuel that you are providing for your mind and body. Simple tasks are going to feel a lot harder and more overwhelming to accomplish. This can make you even more depressed as you see that you are unable to do the things that you used to do before. It becomes a diffi-cult and dangerous cycle that can be hard to free yourself from.

The people you surround yourself with during this time are going to make a big impact on your recovery whether you are experiencing grief or depression. If you keep the people who care about your well-being close to you, they will be there to remind you to take care of yourself and to help you get enough nutrition throughout your days.

It is surprising how the influence of those around you can truly help you because you will start to mirror their behavior. It is no surprise, though, that those you spend the most time with become a part of you in many ways. Their habits and personality traits are bound to rub off on you because you are around each other so much.

Weight Loss

This symptom directly relates to your loss of appetite. Because you are not consuming as many calories as before, you lose weight as you cycle through the grieving process. This weight loss can happen quickly, but it should eventually plateau. Just as you will start to regain your hunger and be able to get a good night's sleep again after some time, you should also start to regain any weight that has been lost as you were mourning. This is an indication that you are following a path of grief.

When you are depressed, the weight falls off quickly and easily. A lot of people are shocked to see that they might still be eating, yet the number on the scale keeps getting lower. This can impact you in many different dangerous ways. Weight loss due to depression can either hinder your self-esteem or excite you because of the unintentional results that you see. An individual might feel embarrassed that they have lost so much weight, becoming a shell of who they used to be. Feeling physically weak can also lead to more emotional weakness.

You may be on the other end of the spectrum and excited by the weight loss. This is a symptom that is trying to turn into an unhealthy coping mechanism. With all eating disorders and related disorders that often stem from depression, the main topic is control. When you see yourself losing weight because you are not eating as much as you once were, you feel that you can control something happening to you in your life. Since you were unable to control the loss of your loved one, this makes you feel better because it acts as a placeholder for all of the control that you thought you had lost permanently.

When you are grieving and depressed, your mind will grasp at any other habits, thoughts, or behaviors to focus on other than the painful reality that you are left to face. Becoming too involved with your recent weight loss can get dangerous quickly. It is important to accept help when it is offered to you or to reach out to someone if you can see that the symptom is becoming too much for you to bear. Other people in your life are probably going to take notice of this physical change, and it is hard to listen to their advice when it is only going to sound like criticism to you.

Open your mind to the idea that these people just want to help you because they care about your well-being. They do not want to see someone they love deteriorate in front of their eyes. With depression, you might not be able to care about this and will continue on your path without food. An intervention is often necessary because this ends up putting you at risk of physical harm. Your body will start to shut down if you stop feeding it, and this is going to debilitate you for obvious reasons.

There are always resources that you can seek if you feel too embarrassed to accept help from the people in your life. Your health and mental health are both so important, and you should never feel ashamed if you reach a point where you admit that one or both are out of your control. There are ways that you can get your life back on track without putting yourself in dangerous positions.

THE DIFFERENCES

There are a few key differences between grief and depression. Below, you are going to explore them so you can become familiar with what each one looks like. By having this awareness, you are taking an additional step toward your healing by ensuring that you are being as safe as possible.

Diagnosis

When you are experiencing a normal phase of grief, you are not officially diagnosed with an illness or an ailment. While you know that grief can take a major toll on your life, it is a normal response to have when you discover you have lost someone you care about. As you are going through grief, all of the symptoms that come with it are going to assist you during your healing. As you cycle through each stage, you will learn how to become stronger and how to successfully manage your grief. In the long run, you are going to learn how to turn your grief into a healing experience.

Before you can feel like you are back to normal, you must explore all of the elements of your grief and where it takes you. While this might be difficult and uncomfortable in many ways, it is encouraged that you explore these feelings as much as you can. When you can get to the bottom of your emotions, you will have a better idea of how you can process them.

This is the foundation for grief and grieving. Since it is a process, you already know that it can take any given amount of time. This is where things can become unclear as to whether you are experiencing normal grief or whether you are going through depression. As time goes on, you may start to wonder if what you are feeling is still falling in line with the typical cycles of grieving.

It is important to check in with yourself often. Understand how you are feeling and why. Consider if any of your symptoms are debilitating you in any way. You do not need to completely stop working or eating to be impacted by your grief. Debilitation can come in the form of ignoring other responsibilities or important regular tasks, such as keeping up with cleaning your house or showering each day. Neglecting habits that keep you healthy and safe could be an indication that your grief is evolving into something further like depression.

While you are grieving, do not stress yourself out by constantly analyzing your behaviors. You do want to monitor them, but not in a way that is going to make you feel overwhelmed or uncomfortable. Be as open and honest with yourself as possible. This is why it is essential to let your thoughts and feelings out through a healthy coping mechanism. When you can unleash what is on your mind, you will be able to better analyze if you are simply going through grief or if you are developing a depressive disorder that is proving to be hard to manage.

No matter how bad each stage of grief gets, you should generally feel that you have everything under control. While your life might feel as though it is spiraling, deep down, you know that it is not. You understand that this is only a temporary part of your life and that you will successfully make it through. Understanding this indicates that you have a healthy grasp on your healing process and that you should cycle through the stages of grief successfully.

Depression is a diagnosed condition. You can find it in the *Diagnostic and Statistical Manual, Volume V* (DSM V). This is the guide that mental healthcare professionals use to diagnose their patients. According to the manual, some of the most common symptoms of depression include:

- Worthlessness
- Extreme guilt
- Suicidal thoughts
- Low self-esteem
- Powerlessness
- Helplessness
- Agitation
- Loss of interest in pleasurable activities
- Exaggerated fatigue

You might feel a lot of these symptoms as you are grieving, but they do not last for an extended period. If the problems you face are ongoing, then this might be an indication of something more serious taking place. The only way to get an official diagnosis for depression is to consult a professional. It is not wise to self-diagnose because this can cause your symptoms to become exaggerated due to worry. Still, you need to pay attention to the way you are feeling, especially if you have recently been having thoughts of suicide.

Another difference between depression and grief is that depression can be dangerous. If you are continually feeling so low, your life might be in jeopardy. Depression causes you to become unable to think clearly, only focusing on what is upsetting you. When this happens to someone who is also grieving, the difficulty can feel like too much to bear. This is why people will often think about suicide as a way to end the pain and suffering. It might seem easier to be gone than to have to deal with the reality of your loved one being gone. No matter what is going on in your life, suicide is not the answer.

If you begin to feel the above symptoms for an extended period, talk to someone. Even if you do not feel that it will help you, reaching out to someone is necessary during this time. Knowing that you are not alone can help to lift you out of the hole you feel that you are in right now, as can psychotherapy. Of course, a mental healthcare professional needs to evaluate you before establishing the best treatment plan.

When you are depressed, your daily routine will often seem incredibly difficult for you to complete. From dropping the kids off at school to getting your work done, this can seem like a hard thing to ask of you during this time. When you think about the loved one you have lost and you have depression, you might be met with feelings of emptiness. This usually occurs because your brain is trying to protect you from the pain of their loss. Instead of being able to look back on warm memories with this person that you cherish, you can only suppress them until you no longer feel anything. Instead of reminding yourself about the good times you had, your brain begins to attack your psyche.

If you have depression, you should not feel ashamed, weak, or unstable. Depression forms due to a chemical imbalance in your brain. Because you are physically unable to give your brain the necessary hormones it needs to feel happy, it takes on sadness instead. Depression is difficult to fight, but you can get through this. If you have been diagnosed with depression or you feel that you would like to talk to someone about it, remember that you are not alone.

Depression is not something that typically resolves itself like grief will. It is a mental illness that has the likelihood of getting worse before it gets any better. Your depression is often going to look like a downward spiral until it feels like it is too overwhelming to bear. If you have any doubts about whether or not you are experiencing depression or regular grief, it is a good idea to talk to someone about what you are going through.

Persistence

As you now know, grief is something that will usually resolve itself over time. You are still going to cycle through its stages, and some of them will be challenging and uncomfortable, but this is normal, and you can work through it. As you experience different feelings and emotions, you learn how to cope with the loss of the one you love to get back to a functional version of your life. This does not mean you are forgetting about them or "moving on." You can still fondly remember your loved one while also living a successful life.

You might feel like it is not okay to be happy while you are grieving, but think about the life you still have left to live. Consider how everything changed in an instant for the person that you lost and how they would probably want you to continue to live your life to the fullest. No day is ever a guarantee, so you need to make the most of each one while you still can. Grief isn't always going to feel this simple, but this is the goal that you should be aiming for, all while focusing on your emotions and working through them with healthy coping mechanisms.

During the first few weeks, you might not feel any different. It might even become apparent that nothing has changed with the way you feel. This is normal. Most people do not feel a shift until they have been grieving for some time. One day, you are going to wake up and realize that it is okay to be happy again. You are going to fondly remember your loved one and the time that you got to spend with them instead of dwelling on the fact that you have lost them. While it won't be easy, the process will teach you how to calm yourself down and refocus your energy on happier thoughts.

Healing happens in waves. You might feel like you are getting a lot better, only to experience a bad day where you feel that you are right back at the beginning of your grieving. This is also normal and happens because healing isn't linear. You might have bad days even years from now, but you will get through them, just like you got through your loss. The best way to make sure that you grieve as long as you need to is by listening to your feelings. If you feel like there are unresolved emotions that you need to address, do so gently. Be kind to yourself as you work on navigating through them and potentially getting the help that you need.

When you have depression, you might also have good days and bad days. The difference here is that you are still depressed daily. No matter how good your day is, there is still a lingering feeling of sadness that won't go away. You might feel like you are running away from your pain and sadness, only for it to catch up with you eventually. There is also the possibility that you will go through measures of distracting yourself or seeking out unhealthy coping mechanisms to feel less sad.

Just because the issue is out of sight does not mean that it is out of mind. If you suppress your feelings, they are bound to come back to the surface at any given time. It might take a small trigger for you to realize that you have yet to process any of your grief and that you must start from the beginning. Depression is great at masking your true feelings because it causes you to become numb. No matter how hard you try, you might still find that you are not getting to the real root of the problem.

Your depression can become persistent, nagging at you daily. Even if you only feel it in small ways, these will add up a lot over time. Everything from the way you talk, act, and think will be impacted by your depression if you allow it to completely take over your life. It is a mental illness that thrives on persistence and longevity. You can feel depressed for so long that you end up believing this is your new normal. But life does not have to feel this way any longer. There is hope, and there are resources you can use to get help.

There tends to be a stigma that surrounds talking to a therapist and getting help for your mental health because physical health is usually made a priority. Just because you cannot see a cut, scrape, or bruise does not mean you aren't in pain. Your mental health matters just as much as your physical health, and you should take it seriously despite what anyone else might think about you.

Nobody else gets to tell you how to heal or what to do regarding your mental health. It is a personal decision for you to make because only you know what you are going through. While depression might be a constant in your life at the moment, you will find ways to work through it and to replace it with other fulfilling elements. You will no longer feel dependent on your sadness, and you will finally be able to live a life that is free of the hardship that your depression has put you through. No matter who you lost or how long ago they passed, depression does not discriminate. It can appear when you least expect it, causing you a lot of mental strain. Be easy on yourself during this time.

While depression is sometimes inevitable during this process, this does not mean you need to feel discouraged or upset with yourself. So many people struggle with their mental health, even those who are incredibly strong. Admitting that you have a problem does not make you weak, nor should it make others think any less of you. If you feel that you are in over your head, there are ways to correct this problem and get your life back on track after you experience your grief.

COMPLICATED GRIEF SYNDROME (CGS)

There are instances where your regular grief can transform into something more severe known as complicated grief syndrome or CGS. The main difference between regular grief and CGS is that the latter is acute and can cause long periods of suffering for the person going through the loss. Some medical professionals suggest that CGS stems from an attachment disorder, which is what happens when you have an intense and long response to a stressor. In the past, doctors avoided treating people who displayed signs of CGS because it was technically a subcategory of grief. While not everybody experiences it, the result is usually still one that ends in healing.

Today, doctors look at CGS differently. Since CGS closely resembles a disorder, they are more willing to look into treatment options for those who cannot withstand their symptoms. Doctors used to view grief as a personal matter that did not necessarily require medical treatment, but through CGS, they are now discovering that it can make you feel similar to depression. You might experience feelings of worthlessness or helplessness, even becoming suicidal. CGS can be dangerous, and it should always be taken seriously.

Some symptoms of GCS include:

- Powerful pain at the thought of your lost loved one

- Heightened focus on reminders that you have lost a loved one
- An overall feeling of numbness
- A feeling of bitterness
- A loss of purpose/motivation
- A loss of trust in other loved ones

If these symptoms last for months after you have lost your loved one, you likely need to seek medical help from a professional.

Looking at these symptoms, some of them resemble what you typically experience as you go through grief. They can also mirror certain depression symptoms. A difference with CGS is that the pain leaves you in a hyper-alert state of being. There are lows, but there can also be intense periods of emotion (bitterness and loss of trust). The moods you experience while going through CGS are more up and down than regular grief or depression.

Even if you are experiencing both CGS and depression symptoms, these are two different ailments that must be treated differently. Many people are quick to assume that it is just one or the other or maybe that something is a normal part of grief. You know yourself better than anyone, and you know how you feel deep inside. If you have any inkling that something is not right, tell someone. Seek help before you are overcome by your sadness. It is never too late to ask for help, even if you have been experiencing these symptoms years after your loved one has passed.

If you do end up being diagnosed with CGS, understand that this does not mean your chances of feeling better have diminished. You might just have to take some additional steps to get there. You cannot control if you develop the syndrome or if you follow a more standard path of grief, so you should never punish yourself for the way that you must heal.

Healing is personal, so never compare your journey to someone else's. Each one is different, and neither is wrong.

3

THE FIVE STAGES OF GRIEF EXPLAINED

To better understand the grief you are going through, it helps to take a look at a model created by Dr. Elisabeth Kübler-Ross, author of *On Death and Dying*. Her influential work, which was inspired by her time with dying patients, has helped many to understand both the five stages of grief and the feelings of those who are about to pass on. While the Kübler-Ross model of grief was first introduced in 1969 when there were few resources on the subject, it is still relevant today.

I will be touching more on this in the coming chapter but although these stages are a great guide, grief is a very personal experience and it can be unpredictable. Don't be dependent on the stages and know that the structure will most likely vary from person to person. Just be open to each stage and be gentle on yourself if things aren't moving as quickly as you intend.

THE STAGES

These stages of grief have already been mentioned briefly, but this chapter will further break down each step according to the Kübler-Ross model. This model was created to help those who were dying to cope with the reality of the situation and was meant to ease the process and help them feel at peace with letting go. The model was then used to help the family members and loved ones of the person who had passed on. Many refer to these stages by the acronym DABDA.

Denial

"This is a mistake."

When you first find out about the loss of your loved one, it is common to refuse to believe the information because it is so shocking and upsetting. This is a defense mechanism that protects you from feeling sad. When you are in this period of disbelief, you usually do not mourn or show much outward emotion because you truly cannot comprehend the loss.

Although you are in denial outwardly, your brain is trying to process the information you were just given. It is cycling through all of the possibilities, like if the news is true or not, and working in overdrive to attempt to make sense of it all. This denial stems from the inability to be fully prepared for a loss. In some cases, you might have a loved one in your life who is terminally ill, but even then, you cannot predict the exact moment when you will lose them.

A common misconception is that you should prepare for the death of your loved ones before they happen to avoid the denial stage. Remember, though, that the stage of denial is necessary and normal to experience. If you try to skip this stage, you will inevitably come back to it in the future. The best thing you can do is to enjoy your life and your time with your loved ones. When a loss does occur, let your brain respond naturally. You might be in denial for a time, but this will soon pass.

Denial ends when you realize that they are truly gone. It might take a visit to the person's home or attending their funeral to fully realize this. When you do reach the point where you can see that you've been in denial, do not punish yourself. You cannot control how your brain reacts to stimuli, and it was simply trying to protect you. What you can do is focus on moving forward to the next stage of grief. You are about to deal with the bulk of emotions that have risen to the surface.

Anger

"This is unfair!"

Reaching the anger stage of grief is an indication that you have accepted the loss. However, this does not mean that you have worked through all of the emotions surrounding it. Anger is usually the next emotion that surfaces because it is a strong emotion. You do not want to give in to the sadness that threatens to take over because you have lost your loved one, so instead, you resort to anger.

The anger that you feel will not necessarily manifest in the way that you think it might. It may be targeted toward yourself, blaming your presence or lack of presence for the loss. You might wish that you had done more or spent more time with your loved one. It is common for regrets to form during this stage.

The anger may also be directed toward other people in your life. Even if they have done nothing wrong and have nothing to do with the loss of your loved one, you might still find it easy to unintentionally take it out on them. Because you know that you have people in your life who love you unconditionally, there is usually no fear that they will leave you. Therefore, it becomes easy to subconsciously take your anger out on them. This can manifest in the way you speak and behave. You might be harsher than usual and less pleasant to be around because of it.

There is another unique way that your anger can appear: anger at the person who passed away. Though they are no longer here, it is normal to be mad at them for passing away. This can be a conflicting feeling because you are sad that they are gone, but you also feel intense anger over that. You understand that it wasn't their choice, but you still feel mad that it happened.

Bargaining

"If only they hadn't gotten into the car."

The bargaining stage of grief is like the "what if" stage. You begin to question if things would have gone differently if your loved one had made different choices. You might even question what you could have done differently to prevent their passing. Deep down, you probably already know that nothing you could have said or done would have saved them, but it is still an overwhelming sensation to think about the possibilities. This is especially true if the loss was traumatic or accidental. Death always teaches us that you never know what is going to happen and when. Life can be so unpredictable, sometimes in jarring ways.

If you believe in a higher power, you may bargain with them. You might pray that they take this news back in exchange for you being a better or more devoted person. While you know that this is not how life and death work, you still desperately try anything you can to revoke the bad news you received.

Bargaining is similar to denial, but there is action involved. You are actively trying to stop the news from being true, and you are willing to make changes or think about other possibilities. This stage of grief can cause you to act differently in an attempt to remedy the situation.

There is no telling how long you will be in the bargaining stage or when it will appear, but remind yourself that you must be willing to let go of the things you cannot control. If you stress over factors that are far outside of your control, you are going to become sick with worry and stress. Letting go is hard, but this does not mean you are letting go of your loved one or the memories that you have of them. By understanding that you are not in control of any one person's mortality, you can move forward in your mourning process.

Depression

"My reason for living is gone."

While you have learned a lot about depression as a mental illness, it also exists as a normal stage of grief. As you already know, the difference is typically within the longevity of the symptoms. Your depression during grief might last for a long time as sadness is a prominent emotion. However, it should start to dissipate over time. You should be able to notice a difference in the way you are feeling, and ultimately, the time that passes will allow you to heal.

However, while you are in the depression stage of grief, life might feel like it isn't going to be okay ever again. At this point, reality has fully set in. You know that your loved one is gone and that there is nothing you can do to change this. All of the emotions that were once bottled up during the earlier stages are now able to come out. This can result in a lot of sadness and emptiness. You might feel that there is a physical space that is missing from within due to the loss of your loved one. This sadness can quickly lead to depression in the form of a mental illness if you do not take care to check in with yourself.

No matter how long this stage lasts for you or how many times you return to it during your grieving, accepting that you feel down is going to help you get through it. You have just lost someone important to you, and it is not realistic to expect yourself to put on a brave face. Loss is scary, hard, and uncertain. It is okay to feel that you are not okay right now. What will get you through this time is knowing that you can heal and feel okay again. This is not forever, and anything that impacts you to such a degree is bound to make you stronger in the long run.

Acceptance

"They are gone, and I miss them."

Reaching the point of acceptance does not automatically mean that you no longer feel sad or upset that your loved one has died. Instead, it means that you have cycled through your emotions and come to the conclusion that you must continue to live your life, even if you still miss and remember them every day. Because accepting their passing does not mean that you need to push their memory aside, your life can be abundant and still full of all of the wonderful times that you spent together. There will be moments when the sadness comes back, but this should not last for too long.

It is okay to cry if you feel like crying, even if you feel that you are at the acceptance stage. Cycling through grief does not mean you are losing any progress. Instead of feeling like you are going backward, acknowledge what you are feeling and try to get to the bottom of it. Often, certain events can trigger you into cycling through the stages. For example, if you wake up feeling extra sad on this person's birthday, you might end up thinking about them and how angry you are that they are not around to celebrate. This is completely normal, and it will probably happen on more than one occasion. Still, you have reached acceptance because you understand the reality of the situation.

Acceptance does not always feel good, but it can lead you to moments that do feel good by honoring and remembering your loved one in the best way possible. At this stage, talking about them usually brings you more joy than sadness or anger. Your mood swings will have leveled out by this point, and you will start to feel more stable. Since dealing with a loss can impact every area of your life, you will slowly start to see things return to normal. You will be able to work through your usual routines with no problems, and everything will fall back into place, as it should.

OTHER GRIEF MODELS

The Kübler-Ross model is not the only model for dealing with grief. After Kübler-Ross passed away, other experts came forward to further expand on the grief model, even making their own. Some prominent researchers who released their information include John Bowlby and Murray Parkes. Bowlby's Attachment Theory and Parkes's Four Stages of Mourning are still widely recognized today, much like the Kübler-Ross model.

Bowlby's Attachment Theory

John Bowlby was a British psychologist and psychoanalyst who was credited with creating his attachment theory. This theory surrounds the idea that the attachments we make early in our lives impact us well into adulthood. Bowlby believed that these attachments influence our mental and developmental health. With the help of fellow psychologist Mary Ainsworth, he came up with this theory that explains the various attachment types and why they form.

Overall, Bowlby believed that children are biologically programmed to seek out and remain close to attachment figures, such as their parents and guardians. When they are close to these individuals, they are given comfort, guidance, and nurturing. These figures are some-what responsible for the child's survival, and by staying close by, the child knows that they are dependent on them.

During his early work, Bowlby worked with children. He was mainly interested in the subject of child development and what would happen if the child was taken away from their caregiver. He wanted to see how this would impact the child's developmental health.

His definition of attachment was that the child and the parent shared "lasting physical connectedness." Bowlby firmly believed that all babies need this type of bond with a caregiver starting in the infant stage because it increases the child's ability to survive. Because babies are born with the ability to cry and coo, Bowlby also believed that caregivers were programmed to naturally respond to these cues. For example, if a baby is crying, the caregiver will pick them up to soothe them.

Even though parents are typically seen as the primary caregivers in an infant's life, there are other attachment figures that this logic applies to. Whether it is another family member or a close family friend, if the infant grows up knowing this person, they have a chance to form a close bond with them. Anyone who provides security and comfort can become an attachment figure in the baby's life.

Bowlby made sure to note that feeding was not one of the reasons for bonds to form. Even without feeding the baby, which is still necessary for survival, you can become an attachment figure by simply providing that feeling of safety and security.

The following are the stages in which attachment forms, according to Bowlby's theory:

1. **Pre-Attachment**: Babies recognize their primary
   caregiver(s) at this stage. However, they have not yet formed
   an attachment to them. As they start to learn how to live in

the world by crying and fussing to express themselves, the attentiveness of their caregiver(s) will show them what love and nurturing is. This is a rewarding experience for both the little one and the parent(s). This stage continues until the baby is around three months, then they recognize their primary caregiver(s) in a way that feels secure and trusting.

2. **Indiscriminate Attachment**: Infants begin to show a preference for their primary caregiver(s) at this stage. They might only be soothed while crying when a parent or guardian tends to them. Even if other adults in their life are capable of the same kind of care, the bond already exists with the primary caregiver(s). That is not to say that the infant will not form close bonds with other caregivers in their lives. If a person is a constant in their lives, they will take a liking to them as well. Trust will be formed on a secondary level to the primary caregiver(s).

3. **Discriminate Attachment**: At this stage, the child has preferences as to whom they trust and wish to be around. They have a strong bond with their caregiver(s), and if they become separated, they might even experience some separation anxiety because they are nervous that they do not know when their caregiver is coming back. An example of this would be when a parent puts their child in daycare because they have to go to work. The child might have a hard time adjusting at first because they are not with their usual caregiver, and they might become fussy and cranky until they can be reunited.

4. **Multiple Attachment**: The child is growing up, but they

still hold a preference for their primary caregiver(s). This is an explorative stage where the child will take an interest in getting closer to other adult figures in their lives. This can be a teacher, a family friend, or other relatives. If those figures are around the child enough, a bond will form that slightly mirrors the bond of the primary caregiver(s). Because the child was introduced to nurturing and care as an infant, they know how to form bonds with other adults in their lives as they grow up.

Thinking about this differently, what might happen if a baby grows up without enough care? Unfortunately, neglect occurs. If a baby is not picked up when they cry or is not cared for when they soil their diaper, they learn that nobody is going to tend to them when they are in distress. The baby will likely grow up with a distrust of adult figures in their lives, even possibly extending to a distrust of other people when they are adults. Their bonds with their caregivers are not strong, and the feeling becomes mutual.

Extreme neglect does not have to be present for a child to lack in this developmental region. In some cases, a baby simply may not take to a parent. Fortunately, there are ways that this can be fixed. The parent might need to spend more time with the baby while being more attentive. Skin-to-skin contact can also create a moment of bonding that cannot be duplicated after the child is out of the pre-attachment stage.

Bowlby's theory suggests that your earliest attachments create the framework for the rest of your life. This is why early childhood development became his passion. He understood that the bond needs to happen sooner rather than later. Otherwise, it becomes more difficult.

The Four Patterns of Attachment

You might be familiar with a term known as "attachment style." It is used for both children and adults and refers to the way you bond with other people in your life. According to Bowlby's theory, this pattern is likely to stay with you if it is the one you grew up with.

Understanding your attachment style can teach you a lot about how you manage your grief and how you experience loss. It further proves that some things are outside of your control, but you can learn to work with them.

Here are the four patterns:

1. **Ambivalent**: This type of attachment happens when a child is distressed after a parent leaves. The separation anxiety impacts them in a debilitating way because their primary caregiver is unavailable. It is a fairly uncommon attachment style to maintain. However, if a child grows up knowing that a parent is too busy to care for them or does not seem to prioritize them, they have a hard time trusting and relying on other people as adults.

2. **Avoidant**: As the name suggests, children with this attachment style tend to avoid their caregivers. They have no preference between one or the other, and they treat a stranger the same way. This is usually the result of abuse or neglect. Because they were shown early on that the primary

figures in their lives are not going to care for them or keep them safe, the children become distrustful of everyone around them. To deal with this, they typically avoid asking for any help or advice. In adults, this attachment style comes off as independent at first glance. On the inside, however, the person might want to reach out but does not know how or is afraid of rejection.

3. **Disorganized**: This is probably the most confusing of the four attachment styles. A child will appear disoriented or confused, and there might be some avoidance or resistance of the primary caregiver(s). It is usually an indication that the child did not properly bond with the parent(s). While they might still provide the child with security and work on nurturing them when they can, there is a slight disconnect in the way that the child feels about them. This is why the behavioral pattern can read in many different ways. In adults, the person might be hard to get close to or make impulsive decisions regarding their social or romantic lives because they do not know how to follow a set attachment pattern.

4. **Secure**: A secure attachment type is the one to strive for. This looks like a child becoming distressed when separated from their parent(s) and feeling joy once they are reunited. When distress is involved, it is not debilitating as it would be in an ambivalent attachment, and there is a balance where the child understands who cares for them and that they have someone they can rely on in their lives. They know that their caregiver(s) will come back for them if they have to be apart. With a secure attachment style, the child feels comfortable

seeking guidance and nurturing from their caregiver(s). This makes for an adult who knows how to express themselves and what they need.

The attachment types further showcase the importance of forming healthy bonds with caregivers at a young age. Since these patterns begin at birth, caring for a child will shape them for the rest of their lives. If you feel that you have developed a negative or difficult attachment style, you can now see that this is not your fault. Everything that happened to you began before you had any autonomous control.

Parkes's Four Stages of Mourning

Bowlby's Attachment Theory was not centrally focused on grief. While it can explain a lot about the human psyche, it is more of an indicator of how early childhood development impacts you as you reach adulthood. It was only later when Bowlby's work caught the attention of grief psychologist Dr. Murray Parkes that a model emerged that was grief-centered. This model is known as the Four Stages of Mourning or the Four Phases of Grief. The foundation of this model is surrounded by the idea that attachment is broken when you lose a loved one. The way you react after this happens is a natural human response and includes:

Shock and Numbness: You can expect these two feelings immediately following the loss of a loved one. Parkes's model suggests that this occurs because you are not yet ready to process the death or accept that it happened. Like the denial stage when talking about the standard model of grief stages, you become keen on protecting yourself from the pain of the loss. This defense mechanism is triggered with little warning, and you often have to sort through it for a while before you can move on to the next stage.

What your mind needs is instant gratification. Understandably, a loss is painful and shocking, and your brain does not want to feel this pain, even for a minute. You may be left unable to cry, which is completely normal because you can't process your emotions. You remain shocked and numb until something breaks you down, allowing you to experience your true feelings.

Again, there is no set amount of time that you will stay in this stage. People cope with loss differently, so the responses are diverse. You cannot force yourself to feel a certain way if you simply do not, so try not to be hard on yourself if you think you are not mourning in the same way as those around you. This is a personal experience, and it is going to be treated as such. You need to do what you can to come to terms with the loss on your own time. Cry if you feel like it, remember the person if you feel like it, and openly discuss it if you feel like it. There should not be too much pressure placed on your shoulders in the beginning; it will only make you feel more resistant to the end goal of acceptance.

Yearning and Searching: This is a time when you likely feel lost and baffled that this could happen to the person you love. The confusing thoughts will likely keep you awake at night as they replay in your head. You might begin to question your mortality and the mortality of those you care about. Each day, you yearn for the one you lost, wishing that they could somehow be brought back to you. Even if you know that this isn't possible, you still put a lot of time and energy into thinking about this.

This stage, which is often accompanied by anxiety and anger, can feel consuming. Throughout this time, you are likely to feel tired and lethargic, and your daily routines are probably more difficult than before. Doing the bare minimum here is usually all that you are capable of. You have just lost a loved one, so do not be too hard on yourself. If you can only do a little bit, celebrate your small accomplishments. Forgive yourself for not being able to operate at 100% like you used to. This is the point of mourning; it is a period where you shift your focus to fully accept the loss of your loved one.

You will likely do a lot of internalized thinking. Even if you cannot share these thoughts with other people yet, you will think deeply about searching for meaning. Whether you are thinking about the meaning of life as a whole or the meaning behind why your loved one was taken from you, this becomes a point where you are likely to appear outwardly pensive. If others ask you if you need anything or if you are okay, remember that they have good intentions. You might still be resistant to help, but make sure that you can see that you still have good people in your life who want the best for you.

Disorganization and Despair: Once you move into this phase, you will feel an abundance of emotions. This can feel especially intense if you were closed-off in stage one. Once you begin to accept the reality of the loss, all of the feelings that were formulating in your brain are going to rise to the surface. They may surprise you as you cycle through various ones each day. One day, you might wake up feeling sad and down. The next, you might feel angry at those around you. Because of this, the most realistic solution for you might be to withdraw from others in your life. Whether you don't want to hurt them or feel that you cannot interact with them, you are at risk of isolating yourself.

Withdrawal often begins during this stage. If you usually have hobbies and habits that keep you happy or entertained, you might notice yourself stepping away from them. While it is ideal to keep yourself occupied in positive ways that will promote positive coping mechanisms, it isn't always easy to continue your life the way that it was before you lost your loved one. Every little thing is likely going to start reminding you of this person, and this can make routines difficult.

It isn't uncommon to seek a change during this phase of grief. You might want to take up a new hobby, spend time around different people, or even change something about your physical appearance. Anything that separates your sadness of the loss from the person you are now will help you cope.

It is especially important in this stage to pay close attention to the way you are coping. If you are using your coping mechanisms as crutches or excuses not to take care of your responsibilities, this is a sign that you have become too withdrawn. There must be a balance within every phase if you want to move through it successfully. The goal is to reach acceptance, and you can only do this if you have the drive to get through the point that you are currently in. While you may feel stuck and hopeless, there are always ways to pull yourself back up. Use the resources you have around you. If someone reaches out to you, try to respond to them. It will benefit you in the long run, even if it initially pushes you out of your comfort zone.

Reorganization and Recovery: At this point, you recognize that your life is forever changed. You can see that there will be permanent differences in your life now that your loved one has passed away, but you are more accepting of them than you used to be. Some days will still be exceptionally difficult, but you have more strength to get through these bad moments. You understand now that this is your new version of normal, and you might have thoughts about what you can do in your daily life to honor your loved one who has passed on.

Wanting your loved one to be proud of you is a common feeling after you have mourned. This is a point in your life where you might want to change your habits or behaviors to become a better person. In this way, the loss can make you more motivated and productive. It gives you a new perspective to consider about life and what you are doing in it. This point is not an easy one to reach, but it is a worthwhile journey that ends up bringing positivity into your life.

The energy that you feel you lost during the beginning stages of mourning will be renewed. All of the activities and things that you used to love before will start to bring you joy once again. Slowly but surely, your life will feel secure again, and you will reach a point where you can fondly remember your loved one. However, this does not mean you have stopped grieving. You can reach this point yet feel like you still need more time to grieve, and that is okay. Going forward, each moment is going to become easier for you.

Though Parkes's stages of grief are clearly outlined and recognized by many people worldwide, it is still not a universal model that works on everybody who has lost a loved one. Grief is complex in the way that it affects people, and some doctors do not believe that this model applies to grieving individuals because they reject the idea it exists. Due to inconclusive evidence, some psychiatrists completely reject both Parkes's model and Kübler-Ross's model. For example, Russell P. Friedman, executive director of the Grief Recovery Institute, claims that no study accurately showcases the positive evidence that surrounds the idea of grieving (Shermer 2008). He believes that grief is natural and cannot be charted with bullet points and milestones.

Robert A. Neimeyer, a University of Memphis psychologist, feels the same way about the subject. He wrote a book, *Meaning Reconstruction and the Experience of Loss*, which describes grief as a process that has no clear point of "recovery." Despite some studies, he does not see any viable evidence that suggests grief can be charted in a way that would indicate which stage you are on and how far away you are from said point of recovery. While there are many different opinions on the matter, it helps to hear both sides of the topic. Since grief is an entirely personal experience, you might find that the models help you cope with the loss. If they do not, however, there is no need to fret since they are not universal or guaranteed.

While many different theories and models have been formed to describe the process of grieving, there is one commonality; it happens in stages. No matter which model you believe in, you are going to have to work through your own experiences to determine what makes you feel better and what will allow you to move on to the next stage.

4

FINDING SOLACE IN STOICISM

There is a branch of philosophy called Stoicism that can help you find solace within your grieving period. Through the Stoic principles, you will be able to feel happier, more resilient, and wiser. This philosophy has helped me conquer many obstacles in my life and the wisdom is timeless and relevant even to this day.

Beginning around 340 BC in ancient Greece, Stoicism is a philosophy that is still widely recognized and used. It focuses on how to handle hardship while maintaining a strong exterior. Stoics are often known as being emotionless, but they are simply trained to process their emotions right away rather than letting them linger.

The founding of Stoicism began with a merchant named Zeno, who was shipwrecked as he was traveling to Athens and lost everything on board. The wealthy merchant continued to Athens, where he visited a bookstore and read a book that introduced him to the work of Socrates. He was so inspired by what he read that he sought out other philosophers and became acquainted with the Cynic philosopher Crates and the Megarian philosopher Stiplo. They taught Zeno about philosophy, which changed his life and his outlook on the negative events in his life. He began to see his shipwreck as a magnificent voyage because he was introduced to these viewpoints.

Settling in Stoa Poikile, which translates to "painted porch," Zeno began teaching and leading philosophical discussions. Originally, his followers were called Zenoians, but they eventually became known as Stoics. Zeno went on to found a school that taught people about Stoicism and its principles, including that:

- Nature is always rational.
- The universe operates based on the law of reason, and humans cannot escape its force.
- To live a virtuous life, you must be rational.
- Wisdom is the key virtue you must strive for; the other cardinal virtues stem from wisdom, and they are insight, bravery, justice, and self-control.
- Poverty, death, and illness are not inherently evil.
- You should feel a dutiful reason to seek virtue, not a pleasurable reason.

Nearly every other religious or spiritual school that came before his school was named after its creator, but Zeno's school was an exception. His new way of thinking spread, and many great Stoic philosophers followed him. Marcus Aurelius, Seneca, and Epictetus are among some of the most famous, and their works and wisdom are still referenced to this day.

THE STOICS

MARCUS AURELIUS

Roman emperor Marcus Aurelius was born in 121 AD. By the time Marcus Aurelius reached his teenage years, the current emperor, Hadrian, was childless and close to reaching his death. Hadrian's first choice as a successor had died unexpectedly, so he was made to choose another—Antoninus, the uncle of Marcus Aurelius. Antoninus adopted Marcus Aurelius, and once Hadrian passed away, Marcus Aurelius was next in line to become emperor after Antoninus.

Marcus Aurelius became emperor in 161 AD, and his rule of the Roman Empire lasted for nearly two decades, up until his death in 180 AD. Throughout his reign, he relied on Stoicism to guide him as a leader, particularly during his military campaigns.

During the years of military conflict, Marcus Aurelius wrote himself private notes that centered around Stoicism. These became the backbone of his famous work, *Meditations*, which is one of the best sources of the principles of Stoicism. These private writings helped Marcus Aurelius to pick himself back up during the rough years of conflict, and they are evidence of his inner strength and the virtues that guided him.

Some of the main lessons we can learn today from Marcus Aurelius include:

Practice Virtues You Can Show

If you feel that you lack certain abilities or skills, it is easy to fall into a pit of self-doubt. During this process of losing faith in yourself, you also lose the ability to realize the things that you are amazing at. To combat this feeling, focus on the things that come naturally to you, what you are already good at. This becomes your foundation for any future self-esteem you develop. If you cannot think of anything that you excel at, take the time to write down each skill that you have. No matter how small or insignificant, write it down, and you might see that you are capable of so much more than you realize. It is quick and easy to list off all of the things you cannot do, but when was the last time you told someone about all of the things you can do?

Draw Strength From Others

Marcus Aurelius was no stranger to seeking inspiration from other people in his life. He had teachers and mentors who influenced him throughout his lifetime, and without their influence, he probably would not have grown to become the wonderful Stoic that he was. To gain strength from others, you must be open to the idea that you cannot possibly know everything. Even after a lifetime of studying, observing, and learning, there is always more to discover. Other people have different life experiences from you, and having conversations with them while keeping an open mind will allow you to expand upon your ideas. Allowing new perspectives is how you can draw strength from those you admire most. Having many role models is common for those who follow Stoic principles.

Focus on the Present

Knowing that temptations exist all around us, Marcus Aurelius was a firm believer in controlling your mind. It is easy to use your imagination to think about what the worst outcome of any given situation is, but you can also use it in a way that will help you progress in life. By focusing on the present and what you can control, you will feel more prepared for your future. Many people start to panic at the thought of the future because they are too worried about the factors that might begin to work against them. Your imagination can become a big tool that you can use, but make sure that you are using it in the right way, a way that uplifts you. Crippling fear will paralyze you if you let it.

SENECA

A Roman philosopher and statesman, Seneca became an influential Stoic in the mid-1st century AD. He was born into a wealthy family, and he came from a lineage of other influential people. As a young boy, Seneca was brought to Rome by his aunt. There, he studied to be an orator and learned philosophy. The school he attended was the School of Sextii, which combined Stoicism and Neo-Pythagoreanism. On a great track in life, it seemed like Seneca had a wonderful future ahead.

One of Seneca's first hardships was the decline of his health. To recover, he moved to Egypt where his aunt and her family cared for him. Once he was healed, he made his way back to Rome in the year

31. It was then that he switched paths, starting a career in politics and law. Fairly quickly, he grew to severely dislike the emperor, Caligula, because of their opposing views. They were on such bad terms that at one point, the emperor ordered Seneca to commit suicide, although he later agreed to spare Seneca's life because he stated that it would be a short one.

In the year 41, Seneca was accused of adultery with the emperor's niece. Claudius, the emperor at the time, banished Seneca to Corsica. During this time, Seneca did not succumb to his punishment. Instead, he thrived and wrote *Consolations*. Eventually, he was allowed back to Rome in the year 49 thanks to the emperor's wife's persuasion. He became a praetor, part of the Roman magistrate, and became tutor to the future emperor Nero.

In the year 54, Claudius was murdered, and Nero became emperor. As Nero's tutor, Seneca's importance grew, and he was even responsible for writing Nero's first speech. Despite his success, Seneca was continually accused of various plots by his political enemies. Unlike a lot of politicians at the time, Seneca had a more humane attitude toward slaves, and he aimed for more fiscal and judicial reform. Many did not agree with this, so he quickly became hated.

Eventually, Seneca fell out of favor, and he died in the year 65. Stoicism continued to spread, and Seneca's memory was kept alive through the teachings of the Stoic leaders who came after him. By the time the 16th century arrived, Senecan style prose had become prominent. People who wrote literature, essays, and sermons often used Senecan style to convey their important messages.

Seneca held several beliefs that are still relevant today, including:

Find an Anchor

Seneca was a believer in seeking inspiration from outside sources, who could serve as anchors in life. To find your anchor, you must find a role model. This person is someone who will influence you. When you do not know what decision to make, think about this person and what they might do. Through their principles, it is thought that we can get one step closer to living a good life, a Stoic goal.

Never Be a Slave of Your Wealth

Though Seneca did come from wealth, he did not simply ride on the coattails of his family. He worked hard to get where he was in his political career, and he continued to work hard on his writing until the day he was forced to death. Seneca was always one to ensure that he was not being too influenced by his privilege, which is a great philosophy to keep in mind, even today.

Fight Your Ego

Seneca had a great deal of confidence and self-esteem, but he did not allow this to go to his head. It is important to make sure that we remain humble. Seneca warned others to never give in to indulgence as this would be a certain downfall to the ego.

EPICTETUS

Unlike the other Stoic influences we have covered above, Epictetus was born a slave, proving that Stoicism can be useful to anyone in any stage of life. Though Epictetus had a different upbringing and more hardship than most, he was still able to use Stoic principles to help guide him along the way.

He was born almost 2,000 years ago in present-day Turkey. His owner, Epaphroditus, allowed him to pursue the study of liberal arts, enabling him to learn about a subject that he was passionate about—philosophy. The Stoic Musonius Rufus became his mentor, and his influence guided Epictetus in many ways.

After emperor Nero's death, Epictetus gained his freedom. He then went on to teach philosophy in Rome for over two decades. This path lasted until Domitian became the emperor and banished all Roman philosophers. Not allowing this to stop him, Epictetus fled to Greece where he went on to found his school of philosophy. He put all of his efforts into this school and teaching until the day he died, a prime example of how he did not allow the hardship in his life to overtake his accomplishments and dreams. Even with his upbringing as a slave, Epictetus never gave up on what he was passionate about.

Another difference between Epictetus and other influential Stoics is that Epictetus never drafted any of his work or chose to publish his beliefs. By an amazing stroke of luck, his influence as a teacher lived on through the notes that were taken by his students. These notes show us that Epictetus seemed to always unintentionally take a different path than most. One big lesson learned from this is that you cannot always choose what happens to you, but you can choose to make the most of it. Instead of wasting your time and energy worrying about the things that are already happening, you can take a more productive route.

As always, there are lessons to be learned from this notable Stoic:

Remember What You Have Control Of

This is one of the biggest Stoic principles to remember. Epictetus had nearly every challenge in his life to deter him, but he never allowed this to set him back. He still went on to pursue his dreams because he chose to focus on the elements he had control of.

Some things are simply going to be outside of our control. No matter how much we prepare for certain things to happen, there are still outside factors that can influence the final result. We might believe that we are ready for any of these options, only to be surprised when the situation takes a turn. This is enough to upset or overwhelm the average person, but Stoics train to work with any result that they are met with.

You can only focus on yourself in any situation. Once you have taken all of the necessary precautions, you must use the energy you have left to work on what you can do to improve your life. Think about what you can do to change anything unfavorable, and do not give up because you think that there is nothing more that can be done. There is always more if you look for it.

Set the Standard

Stoicism teaches us that we must be brave when it comes to being open to change. Epictetus did not believe in lecturing people by using persuasion. Instead, he wanted to be a living example of the principles he believed in. He thought that would make a much more convincing argument.

You need to let your actions speak loud and clear. If you have beliefs, you must act in accordance with them at all times. This gives you credibility among those around you. Instead of convincing others to stand by your side, you must set a standard of being that will convince them on their own.

If you are looking for a role model and evaluating different people, consider what put them in this ideal position. It was likely their actions that drew you in. They convinced you to listen to what they had to say and why their viewpoints mattered.

Life is all about the choices you make. If you are unhappy with the choices you have made so far, you can always make changes. You can completely transform your life if you are willing to try something different.

Create Your Character

Habits have a big influence on nearly all humans. Epictetus was aware of this, and he always encouraged his students to break free from the norm.

When we rely on habits too much, we become oblivious to other opportunities that we encounter. Imagine that you are used to driving to work the same way every day. There are other ways you can drive, maybe some that will save you time by avoiding traffic, but you have always used the same route. This is an example of a way that your habits and routines might be holding you back. They are keeping you in a stagnant state of being that makes it more difficult to branch out.

Many things in life define your character, and all of them come together to create who you are as a person. It is not easy to make changes in routines and habits because these are things that keep you feeling secure. They allow you to feel that you are accomplished and safe. Sometimes, though, it is necessary to rattle this feeling of security without fully breaking your spirit. Show yourself that there are other steps you can take to achieve the same results. If you open your mind to these new ways, you might be surprised at what you find.

STOICISM IN MODERN TIMES

While learning about the ancient practice of Stoic philosophy can be interesting, you might be wondering how these principles apply to the world we live in today. You can take some inspiration from Ultimate Fighting Championship (UFC) champion Khabib Nurmagomedov. In less than two rounds in October 2020, he was able to choke out his opponent. This secured his lightweight championship belt. As soon as the fight came to its conclusion, Nurmagomedov collapsed to the ground in tears. This is an unusual sight for a UFC fighter, especially since they are known for their grit and tough demeanor. Later that day, he announced his retirement. Considering that he was ending on a high note, it is easy to see how this could have contributed to his stream of emotions.

On a deeper level, Nurmagomedov was also going through the grieving process. Just three months before the fight, he lost his father. This fight that he had just dominated was the first that he had ever fought without his dad there in his corner. His mom wanted him to stop fighting after this, and he agreed that it would be for the best.

Nurmagomedov did not want to continue now that his father was gone. It was a difficult and bittersweet moment for him as he wept on the floor and later announced his retirement, but he proved his strength and tenacity by giving an impressive battle.

Stoicism often allows people to look strong and powerful on the outside. If you just looked at Nurmagomedov in the octagon, you would have never guessed that he was going through a recent loss. He took all of his courage and focus and channeled it into his fight, and it paid off. After the relief he felt once he won the fight that only he knew was going to be his final one, he was able to release all of the emotions that were being kept inside.

His Stoic approach to managing his emotions got him through all of the suffering he had to endure. Because of the loss of his father, he was placed in a position to either forfeit his fight or to continue. He decided to channel his strength to continue, and it showed him exactly what he was capable of. You will encounter many moments in your life that will ask you to stand strong in the face of adversity. While you might not be fighting in the UFC, you will have to put on that bravery to get you through the moment just like Nurmagomedov did.

STOICISM: DEATH AND GRIEF

The Stoics had a lot to say about death and grief because they are so natural and such a big part of the human experience. Many classic Stoic texts feature the topic of death because it is one of the things most outside of our control. After all, every human has a life that they can choose to live to their fullest, but they typically do not know when it is going to end. This can feel like a daunting thought to many people, especially as they begin to experience the loss of loved ones in their lives. You do not want to live a life that is tethered to the fear of death or dying. Instead, you can take a page from the Stoics' book and learn how to view death as intended—a natural phenomenon.

The Stoics were well known for remembering their mortality. They even had the phrase "memento mori," which translates to "remember death." The Stoics did not want to think about death in a fearful or impending doom type of way. Instead, they aimed to become aware of their mortality and how things could change in an instant. They knew that no matter how successful they were or how well-versed they were in life, they were still going to meet the same fate as every other human on the planet. This can become a comforting thought if you allow it to.

With memento mori as a tool for guidance, the Stoics did not forget about how limited their time on Earth was. Whenever they needed extra motivation to persevere, they considered that their time was not infinite. They needed to pursue their passions sooner rather than later or else they might miss out on the opportunity to do so at all.

Epictetus took this one step further with a somewhat controversial reminder that he told others to keep in mind. He advised people to think about tucking their children into bed at night. Then, he told them to imagine what it would be like if their children were no longer there. Waking up without them would be devastating, and the thought further proves that the Stoic principle of being present in the moment is so important.

Using an "ignorance is bliss" approach was never recommended by the Stoics. While this does keep you free of the fear that can come attached to the idea of death, it leaves you feeling too unprepared when it happens. The shock of this moment can debilitate you if you ignore it until it is happening to you. Open your eyes to the death that surrounds you in your life already. Turn to nature; even the simplest of plants and trees die. This is going to desensitize you to death, in a way.

While there is nothing that can ever truly prepare you for the loss of a loved one, a general acceptance of the nature of death is helpful.

Conquering the Fear

It is within the Stoic belief that we should conquer death by learning how to use it productively. To do so, we must learn how to see it objectively.

Seneca wrote a letter of condolence to his mother, and in this letter, he acknowledged that the rule of Fortune is harsh and unfavorable. He also reminded her that it is now in her control to either endure the suffering or succumb to it. While it cannot always be avoided and while it is not always deserved, we must learn how to power through it to become strong enough to move into the next stage of grief.

A question posed to the Stoics is how to make sense of this harsh reality that can often feel cruel. How does one come to terms with the fact that we are eventually going to lose a lot of people we love and that there is nothing we can do to stop it?

One thing we can do is to stop catastrophizing the concept. Death is terrible and sad, but it does not have to be a looming presence in our lives at all times. When we are not mourning, we must be living. Other things are going to happen in our lives that are going to allow us to feel emotions.

A common misconception about Stoicism that affects grieving is that Stoics do not like to tap into their emotions, that they want people to suppress them. This is not true, though.

The Stoic philosophy teaches us to face our emotions head-on. When we experience a loss or have to deal with death, it is thought that we should begin processing the emotions as soon as possible. This will allow them to pass so they no longer hinder us in life. Running from your emotions only provides you with temporary relief. It all goes back to the "ignorance is bliss" mentality. All of the emotions that you run from will eventually catch up with you. Then, you will have to face them, and you might feel even less prepared to do so.

If you tell other people in your life that you are fine and insist you do not need to talk about your emotions, you are suppressing your feelings. This hinders your healing process and makes you feel like you are being overpowered by the difficult feelings you are struggling with.

Many people seek distractions to get their mind off of the loss, but this can work both to your advantage and disadvantage. Stoicism warns against too much distraction, but a little can prove to be helpful. When you find healthy coping mechanisms that can help to make you feel like yourself again, you will be better able to process the emotions that you are left with.

Face the pain now. If you are going to take one lesson from the Stoics regarding grief, this should be it. Take away any expectations that you have about the process because, much like death, it is not going to be predictable. See where your feelings take you, and understand that it isn't always going to be a smooth ride. It will get easier, though. The more that you process your feelings, the more strength you will obtain. Rely on your inner strength to conquer your grief while remembering that this is a natural part of your life.

More Advice

Seneca urged people to speak with their friends and family members to fondly remember the person who passed away. Through memories shared, this person is kept alive in a way.

But this can be difficult because many people who know you are going through a difficult loss might be unsure of how to approach you. They will be cautious of upsetting you, but if you make it clear that you are willing to talk about fond memories of the person who has died, they will be better able to help you get through this difficult time. Having others to talk to about the person you have lost will provide you with a nice sense of solidarity that counteracts the loneliness you may also feel.

Marcus Aurelius gave some advice in his *Meditations*. He explained that you can be grateful for those important people in your life before they pass away. He started his book with a list of the people relevant to his life, and he urged others to do the same. Before any loss happens, or if it has already occurred, you can make a list of everyone in your life you currently feel grateful for. These individuals can bring you many different positive traits, which help you to live and behave at your best. They also allow you to be your true self because a level of trust is formed that just is not present when you are surrounded by people you do not know well or people who do not have your best intentions at heart.

Thinking about the ancient Stoic times, you can rest assured that these people also dealt with the struggles that come with death and the hardship that comes with grieving. You are not alone in this journey, no matter how much it feels this way. Dealing with death and loss is a part of being a human being, and you can gain inspiration from all of these Stoic individuals who have gone through it before. Harness their strength to get you through your journey.

Negative Visualization

One way that all three of the above Stoic philosophers worked through hard times is by practicing the art of negative visualization. This is a type of visualization that allows you to predict worst-case scenarios before they happen to you. To do this, you must foresee the bad things that could potentially come your way. It takes self-control to do this, of course, because it is easy to overthink the possibilities. The result is going to be more favorable because you will either be better prepared for the bad event or it will not occur.

If this sounds like the opposite of positive thinking, that's because it is. Negative visualization goes against everything that positive thinking stands for. This can be taken as a pessimistic outlook on life to some onlookers, but true Stoicism is not pessimistic. It is a matter of hoping for the best yet preparing for the worst. The Stoics were not frequently faced with disappointment thanks to the art of negative visualization. Because they were always mindful of the potential negative events to come, they were not often caught off guard if they happened.

When you find yourself scared of a specific situation, for example, the loss of a loved one, try negative visualization. You know that death is natural, and it will occur. However, you might not know if you will lose your loved one first or if they will lose you first. Naturally, the thought is unsettling. You can imagine each possibility to better prepare yourself for any outcome. When my mom knew her time was coming to an end, she always told my brother and I we needed to take care of her dog. Although, this thought pained me as our family dog was most attached to her, in a way it helped me imagine my life without her. It was the last thing I wanted, but at this point it was inevitable. It made me think of how I would take care of the dog, talking it on walks and feeding her. This visualization made me a lot less scared and anxious of the future. Although this practice is not ideal, there is some power behind it.

Remember, though, that Stoicism is rational and logical. Do not get too carried away with the negative thoughts, but allow them to guide you to each conclusion. It is like exploring the "what ifs" that always pop into your head. Some might argue that you should simply ignore those thoughts, but addressing them directly can be enough to put them at ease and to remove the fear.

There are several ways you can go about negative visualization if you'd like to try it out in your life. You can picture your daily routine and all of the inconveniences that might occur during it. Think about how you would handle getting caught up in traffic or dealing with difficult clients at work. Maybe you burn dinner and get into an argument with your spouse. Anything can happen, and even if it seems minor, it is still going to impact you.

The other way you can go about negative visualization is to directly imagine the loss that you fear. Think about it head-on, and pay attention to the emotions that this brings forth.

It does take practice to master the art of negative visualization. One positive part of facing depression or depressive symptoms is that it can allow you to better practice this art. Since you are naturally going to be imagining the worst things you can think of, explore these feelings and how to better get ahold of them. You do not need to be brought further down by the thoughts that live in your head; you can rise above them while still paying close attention.

Writings on Death and Grief

While Stoicism lives on today through those who practice it, they learn what they know from the ancient texts written by the great leaders who have passed away. Through reading the writings in this section, you might be able to discover a new outlook on death that does not scare you or impact you in the same way as it used to.

Seneca's *Dialogues and Letters* provides you with a letter that he wrote to console his mother. Her mother died while giving birth to her, which naturally impacted her deeply. His mother was also dealt an unfortunate blow when she found out that her grandson passed away. This happened only days before Seneca was banished from Rome. This specific story is called *Consolation to Helvia.* Seneca shares his musings on grief in this letter, and there is much to learn from it.

While Epictetus did not write in the same way that Seneca did, his teachings have still been compiled into a work called *The Discourses.* Here, you can find his sentiments on the mortality of the ones we love. He guides us through thoughts about the idea of loss, which can prove helpful when we are forced to suddenly let go. Instead of thinking about the loss as a devastating tragedy, Epictetus preferred to think of it as a "sweet sadness" in your heart. This stems from the idea that you can still remember your loved ones fondly, especially after they pass. Their memories will remain alive in your heart.

Of course, Marcus Aurelius' work titled *Meditations* has been referenced several times in this book. It remains a prominent collection of writing that not only explains Stoicism in a great way but also helps you to work through your grief. He talks a lot about life and death and how they relate to one another. When you think about death as a part of a cycle rather than a standalone event, you can broaden your mind to the idea that it is a natural part of life. He provides his readers with great advice on how to get the best start to each of your days and how to live with a sense of honor in everything that you do.

It may seem intimidating to read about grief, especially if you are currently in the thick of it, but each of these writings has a lot to offer, and they are worth exploring.

5

FACE YOUR PAIN AND YOUR GRIEF

To face the pain you feel from the loss you have endured, you must start at the first step—handling your avoidance. There are two different types of avoidance that people typically go through when they discover they have lost a loved one. Some avoid participating in activities that remind them of their loved ones. The memories that arise might be too painful to face because a lot of them are going to be centered around the person who is gone. The second type of avoidance is when you avoid something that once made you happy or will make you happy. There is a sense of guilt that can arise when you are dealing with a loss. The voice in the back of your head might be telling you that you do not deserve to be happy because your loved one has passed away.

There is a third way that grief might be avoided, and it is more subtle. Some people opt for distractions that will keep them busy. This might not seem problematic on the outside, but it is still a method that allows you to avoid thinking about the sadness and pain that you are feeling. This can look like taking on extra shifts at work or immersing yourself in a hobby that prevents you from having too much free time. You might subconsciously begin to stay busy because your brain knows that stillness will bring forth the dark thoughts.

HOW DO YOU KNOW IF YOU ARE BEING AVOIDANT?

You must learn the difference between a healthy distraction and avoidance because the line is subtle. When you are grieving, you are more likely to make decisions outside of your character. This happens because you feel so uncomfortable due to all of the sadness.

Pay attention to the choices that you make during this time. They are going to be telling of how well you are working through your grief. If you notice that you are changing your routines and habits, question yourself. Think about whether or not the things you are filling your time with are helping you and making you happy or simply keeping you occupied so you do not feel overwhelmed. There are moments when the process is going to feel impossible, but you will still be able to find a healthy distraction to get you through it.

For a distraction to be healthy, you must be participating in an activity that lessens the intensity of your sadness and pain. You are not supposed to completely do away with your pain because that is not realistic, but anything healthy for you will help you have a moment to breathe. When using a distraction, be sure to give yourself breaks from time to time so that you can check in with yourself frequently.

The main focus of your healthy distractions should always be your well-being. Ask yourself if what you are doing is benefitting you. If so, in what ways? Identifying this will make it easier for you to determine if you are engaging in a healthy distraction or not.

When you take a little break from your grief, remember that it is only temporary. You will return to it later. The break is not your result but a moment for you to recollect your thoughts. This will lessen the intensity of all of the bad feelings, especially on your hard days.

All of your days might feel like hard days when you first lose someone you love, but this is okay. You can engage in a healthy distraction daily if it helps you. As time goes on, you will find the need to rely on this distraction less and less. Still, you are learning a healthy management technique for your emotions. Activities that allow you to feel rejuvenated will greatly benefit your well-being. Some examples include:

- Breathing exercises
- Yoga
- Meditation
- Massage
- Reading
- Relaxing

Your healthy distraction should also be deliberate; it is something you do by choice and with control. Avoidance techniques are often chosen outside of your control. You might find yourself doing certain things that you do not remember deciding on. This is a key difference between the two actions. Every time you are engaging in a healthy distraction, you should feel positive about it because you chose it for yourself.

The activities that you find healing might differ from those that others find healing. You need to listen to your mind and body to discover which ones are personally restorative to you. Make sure whatever you do does not just provide short-term gratification.

Some activities that you might engage in will only provide you with the feeling of instant gratification. You will feel better at first, but then, your condition will worsen. Shopping to fill a void is an example of one of these behaviors. It might feel great to spend money because it is distracting, but this isn't necessarily restorative to your mental health.

Be wary of the way that you use your healthy coping behaviors as well. While watching your favorite movie can be incredibly healing, watching it late at night and disrupting your sleep pattern can cause you to feel tired at work. You need to keep in mind that there are limits that come along with every behavior, even the healthy ones. Be smart about the way you are caring for yourself and treating yourself. This will directly impact your ability to get through your grief.

Most people imagine relaxing activities when they think about healthy coping mechanisms, but this does not always have to be the case. You can engage your mind in healthy ways, too. Using your creativity during this time can be a great way to get your feelings out. You can paint, draw, write, sing, and act to engage that inner creativity. Exercise is another form of healthy behavior. This one works especially well because it provides you with endorphins simultaneously. These are the happy chemicals that uplift your mood. Experiment with some of these things as a way of including them in your routine again.

If you are still having trouble deciding if an activity is healthy, ask yourself if it is practical. If you find something that you love and that makes you feel great, it is not going to do any good if it drains you of your resources. For example, you might enjoy going out to sing karaoke with friends. This can be a fun thing to do every once in a while, but going every other day is going to drain you of your money and energy. You must still practice self-control, even through grief. Giving in to all of your desires will not help you heal; it will only create more problems for you to fix in the long run.

The last thing you need is to pick up on some bad habits during your grieving process. They are more likely to become permanent fixtures in your life because you are relying on them more heavily than you normally would. While it is hard, you still need to consider your future. Do not make decisions in your life without considering how they will affect you right now and in the future. You can allow yourself to give in to your guilty pleasures sometimes, but you should also know that this isn't going to become a regular habit.

Your healthy distractions will often involve other people. Spending time around other people is a fast and effective way to get your mind off of anything draining. The energy that they bring into your life can help you a lot, and this is why you must make sure you are only surrounding yourself with the best people. Be sure that the people you allow to get close to you have your best intentions in mind. They will want you to be happy, and they should be willing to engage in healthy coping behaviors with you so you do not feel alone. If someone begins to influence you to pick up on bad habits, then this person likely does not have your best intentions in mind. They might mean well, but you need to stand up for yourself and know what is right.

Management Strategies

Now that you are aware of the difference between avoidant behaviors and healthy coping behaviors, you can learn how to help yourself when you are feeling your worst. Remember that avoidant behavior takes more effort than healthy behavior. You will likely spend twice as long thinking about how to avoid unpleasant emotions instead of simply confronting them. Understandably, you are not always going to be able to confront them right away, and that is okay. This is why you should give yourself breaks where you can engage in healthy behaviors.

A pattern that will help you spot avoidant behaviors follows:

Stressful trigger > negative thought and physical response > feeling overwhelmed > avoid activity or thoughts that involve the trigger

When you notice that this is taking place, pause for a second. Take a few deep breaths, then ask yourself these questions:

- What am I trying to avoid?
- What has my current coping mechanism(s) cost me?
- How much time do I spend on avoidance?
- Am I being avoidant due to fear of something or someone?

Next, you need to reflect on your answers. To find a balance, think about a healthy distraction that is short and easy for you to engage in. This should be something that does not deplete you or your resources. While being mindful of the activities you choose, you will notice an improvement in the avoidance pattern that you used to follow.

As you think about the activities you'd like to incorporate into your routine, ask yourself if each one reduces the negativity you are experiencing in your life. See if it makes your hardship easier to manage. If the answer is no, then you should probably move on to the next activity.

You might also be able to come up with a creative resolution that allows you to engage in the activity without straining yourself. For example, again, imagine that going to the karaoke bar with your friends brings you joy. Since this is something you cannot do every day, you might take up singing at home for a few minutes each day. While this is not the same experience, it might be a step in the right direction.

You also need to allow yourself some time to think about solutions. It isn't common to know right away which activities will help you heal. It might take several weeks or even months to come up with anything at all. Do not feel discouraged, and always remain open to suggestions. The people in your life might share advice with you based on what is working for them or what they have done in the past. Since you do not have to go with their suggestion automatically, there is no pressure to act. Simply listen to what they have to say. If this is someone who cares about you, they are likely telling you because they do not want to see you suffering.

Why Avoidance Won't Work

Sadness is not a feeling your brain wants to experience, so it will naturally do everything it can to avoid it. Your mind might choose to focus on ideas that are not relevant to you just so it does not have to feel these unpleasant emotions such as sadness. Most would argue that part of the meaning of life is to find true happiness. This can feel difficult after you have lost a loved one. Since your life now feels different, maybe dark, it is harder to figure out which path you need to take to get to happiness. When you become a prisoner of your dark thoughts, the avoidance comes quickly. Your brain will desperately try to grasp at this method until you can feel a fraction of relief.

It is going to be difficult to break free from this pattern, but you are capable of doing it. You can change your life, even as you are grieving. To do that, though, you must recognize the patterns of avoidance you are relying on. The following are some examples of avoidance and why they do not work. Use them to inspire you to make changes. Seek strength in knowing that there are other ways you can make yourself feel better during this time.

Work or Daily Tasks

The thing about grief is that it is not patient. It will not politely step aside as you go to work and complete your daily tasks. Often, tending to your responsibilities while you are grieving can trigger a lot of avoidance. These tasks are going to feel much harder than they usually do and might prove to be a struggle. On the other hand, you might feel the need to immerse yourself in your work. By taking on extra shifts and more hours, you might believe you are productively handling your grief. As you already know, this is not balanced, and balance is necessary to find a better way to cope with your grief.

If you stop completing your tasks, you are going to be met with a lot of stress. This happens because you have too much free time to focus on your sadness and pain. As the deadlines begin to catch up with you, it will feel incredibly overwhelming. If you choose to over-work yourself, you will not have a free moment to think. While this might feel better than thinking too much, it is still avoidance to a high degree. As you know, there needs to be time set aside for you to ponder the way you feel. The emotions need to be addressed if you want them to pass.

Caring for Others

Caring for other people instead of yourself during a period of grief is common, especially if the person who has passed away left behind a spouse or other family member. It might feel good to do this good deed, but the activity can become immersive and draining in itself. Taking on a caregiver role feels natural to many, and this can be a kind gesture, but you must ensure that you are still keeping your life balanced.

Set boundaries with your emotions. If you feel that you have nothing left to give to other people, then you definitely won't have anything left for yourself. You must always save some time and energy to spend on yourself and your well-being, even if you can only manage one form of self-care. Anything that you were not doing before is going to feel like an improvement.

Drugs or Alcohol

Unfortunately, many people find it easy to abuse substances while they are grieving. This happens because these substances are highly addictive. When mixed with sadness and an addictive personality, the result is not going to be good. If you notice that you are becoming reliant on substances, seek help immediately.

Seeking treatment during this time can be a blessing in disguise. Not only will you be able to work through the substance abuse problem, but you can also learn how to sort through your feelings surrounding the loss. Try to let your guard down if this is the case. It might feel shameful, but getting help is a lot better than letting the problem persist and worsen.

Travel

Traveling can be great when you are feeling stuck in a phase of your life. Getting out of the same environment that you are always in will feel refreshing, but remember your balance; you cannot travel forever. If you find yourself going on back-to-back trips, you might need to slow down and check in with your emotions.

Use travel sparingly as a coping mechanism because it can be a form of escapism. For example, going on a weekend drive into the next town can serve as a great way to promote healing. You can experience a different atmosphere temporarily. When you return to your environment, you should feel rejuvenated and ready to take on your healing process once again.

Isolating

Isolating yourself while you are grieving can come naturally. Since you do not feel like yourself, you might not want to subject other people in your life to this energy. In a way, you will feel like you are doing other people a favor because you do not want to feel like a burden. Taking a little alone time can be a healthy way to sit with your thoughts and address them, but remain mindful of how much time you are taking.

While you don't need to jump straight back into socialization, you should make an effort to see some people in your life who you love. Do not commit to long or complex plans. Sitting down with a friend over coffee to talk can be an easy way to transition into talking to other people. Be easy on yourself, and take your time.

COMMON PATTERNS FOR GRIEF AVOIDANCE

We looked at one avoidance pattern in the previous section, but there are several more to be aware of. These avoidance patterns tend to appear after you lose a loved one, and you will probably be able to identify with one or more of them in the beginning. By paying close attention to them, you will be able to stop any unhealthy behavioral patterns before they enter your daily routine.

The Procrastinator

This type of avoidance revolves around the idea that if you ignore your pain for long enough, the grieving period will pass on its own. While it might feel this way with avoidance, you already know that this is not true. The period of grief isn't passing when you "procrasti-nate" your mourning. It might go away for a while as long as you can keep up with the distractions, but it will return to you when you least expect it.

Grief and sadness are easily triggered. One day, you might see some-thing that reminds you of the person you lost, and all of your memo-ries of that person will come flooding back. This will eventually lead you to the conclusion that they are gone, and you will likely spiral into a wave of depression and dark thoughts. It is an overwhelming burden to take on all at once.

The procrastinator type might believe that giving in to grief is a sign of weakness. Instead of crying and thinking about their emotions, the person might believe that it is better to toughen up. This means that walls are being put up in an attempt to stifle the emotions that are trying to surface. It might seem like this person is incredibly strong, but this is only the case until they are triggered into experiencing their grief.

With this method of avoidance, you have little control over what is happening and when. At any given time, you might feel overcome with emotions. You might even become fearful of when this is going to happen and how you will further postpone your grieving. This is an exhausting way to live and is not a sustainable lifestyle that anyone should have to endure. You already have a limited supply of energy as it is, so there is no need to further drain yourself by doing this.

Understandably, you might not feel like you have a choice in the matter. When grief tries to enter your life, it can become an automated response to procrastinate dealing with it. Always remember that you have a choice; you can make a small change in your life that will completely change the way you feel. It takes strength and bravery to move forward in this way, but you can do this. Give yourself the necessary motivation, and seek inspiration from others who have also been in your situation.

If you do not seek help or make a change, this type of avoidance pattern can evolve into serious depression or other mental health issues. Feeling the weight of long-term depression is going to make your grieving period even harder. Realize that you deserve better than this and that there are always resources for you to seek. If you do not know where to begin, you can always visit your local medical professional for guidance. They will be able to create an actionable plan full of steps that you can take.

The Displacer

This type of avoidance is complex because you go through the stages of grief as expected. You might experience strong emotions, such as anger or sadness, but you will direct them toward other people instead of addressing them on your own. When you do this, you are a displacer. The correct way to handle these emotions is to apply them to the person you are grieving, even the most difficult ones. This is how you are going to be able to sort through them properly.

A few things happen when you misdirect emotions toward other people. You might end up pushing people away who truly care about you. Even if you secretly do want their support, your emotions are going to tell you otherwise. They might make you act out of character in an attempt to self-isolate. You might also anger or upset the good people you have in your life. When you are feeling such intensity and directing it at other people, remarks often get taken to heart. Whether you mean to or not, you might end up hurting someone's feelings.

Keep in mind that this type of avoidance pattern can happen subconsciously or consciously; you might know exactly when you are doing this, or you might never realize it. Being mindful is going to help you in either case. When you are more aware of your actions, you can pick up on the cues that will tell you when you are doing it. If someone is upset or offended by your behavior, think about whether or not they have done anything to wrong you or hurt you. It is often the pain you feel from your grief that likes to lash out at people who love you unconditionally. Subconsciously, your brain is okay with this because they know that these people are supposed to care about you no matter what.

Even if you are not taking your anger out on other people, when you experience this kind of avoidance, you might feel constantly agitated about the smallest things. Every inconvenience is going to feel like a personal attack. If this happens, it will become difficult for you to enjoy your life. This can result in excessive complaining and can often end up pushing others away. You tend to become so self-focused that you forget to check in with those you care about. Any connection that you have in your life is a two-way street, and it takes mutual effort to maintain each one. This avoidance pattern almost makes you feel selfish, but you also feel like you cannot help it.

To reverse this feeling that you have inside, you should set a focus on self-care. When you begin caring about your well-being, the bad feelings you have inside should lessen. Bringing peace and clarity into your life can work wonders for your healing process. It might be uncomfortable to be kind to yourself, especially when you are feeling extremely agitated, but be patient with the process. Think about feeling better, not just right now but also in the long run.

The Substituter

This is a complex form of avoidance because it can happen in stages. You had a unique bond with the person you lost, whether they were your friend, family member, or romantic partner. When you experience the substitute avoidance pattern, you take all of the feelings and emotions you had for the person you lost and transfer them to someone else in your life. This is a hasty way to build any kind of relationship, and it can come off strong to the other person.

You might be so used to certain interactions and moments with the one you lost that they are programmed into your muscle memory. Since you have such a strong urge to continue the routine, you will try to find the next best person to try to have this bond with. By no means are you trying to replace your lost loved one; you are trying to find an outlet for the fondness you are left with. Instead of accepting that this person is gone and the routines you used to have are no more, you will do everything in your power to continue with them. Of course, you know that routines provide you with comfort and safety, which is why the decision is often hasty.

To prevent yourself from falling into this pattern, you can follow the three C's: companionship, commonality, and commitment. This is a good guideline to follow if you notice that you are growing closer to certain individuals in your life. You are probably leaning on them because they provide you with companionship, which can end up being a positive thing. Once you realize you have someone like this in your life, you need to determine if you have anything in common. Is the common link healthy?

Finally, your commitment to this person must be equally matched. This means that the feelings should be reciprocated. If you are invested in a relationship of any kind and the other person is not, you are bound to end up getting hurt. Not only will you feel betrayed when you realize you are putting more effort into the relationship, but you will also be hurtled through the process of grieving your lost loved one when you realize that you cannot simply substitute people to stand in for them.

Accepting that they are gone is hard. It makes sense that your brain would seek out substitution as a valid solution, but you need to consider the real reason behind why you are doing this—remind yourself of the three C's.

When you are substituting as a way of avoidance, you might end up convincing yourself that you are not being as strongly impacted by the loss of your loved one as you thought you would be. This can provide you with a sense of security and control. If there seems to be little risk of being overwhelmed, then you will often continue with the behavior that gives you this security.

The Decreaser

The main goal of this type of avoidance is to decrease the amount of grief that is felt. This can feel like a positive thing at first, but it becomes unhealthy when you end up never processing or addressing your true feelings. There are various techniques that you can rely on to use the act of decreasing your grief as a way of avoidance. People who fall into this pattern will normally become faith-based as they navigate through their grief. They will often find themselves praying, even bartering with the higher power that they believe in. What they seek is strength to overcome the grief and a way to decrease the level of intensity.

One of the main negative elements of this type of avoidance is that you might lead yourself to believe that you are okay, even without cycling through all of the stages of grief. Since you have faith in a higher power and feel that you are being heard, you might not want to seek out other help or treatment for your grief because you believe it is shortly coming to an end. Remember, grief ends with acceptance. This process can last for many years after you experience the loss, and it can continue for the rest of your life whenever you think about the person you lost.

Another worrisome outcome of this avoidance pattern is that people on the outside will think that you are doing fine. They might even be surprised that you are coping so well and believe that you do not need as much support as you do. Putting on a brave face like this is not always going to benefit you in the long run. This is just another way of putting off the inevitable. You need to address all of the moments you experience, even the weak ones.

Using rationalization is a big part of this avoidance pattern. Because you can see that your pain and sadness are decreasing, you might use this as an excuse to stop talking about your feelings or the loss. A little rationalization can be beneficial, but when you are insistent on it, it only fuels your avoidance even more. You can use your rational brain to understand that you aren't going to feel sad forever; there are ways you can find to pick yourself back up. It goes beyond rationalization when you believe that you are invincible or that you do not need any more help.

When it comes down to it, every step of the grieving process is important. You need to go through the hardship of grief to get the full picture of how to survive it. While you are healing, you aren't supposed to feel like you already know how to do everything. Even if you have experienced loss in the past, each one is unique. The whole process is personal, and it should be treated as such.

The Hypochondriac

This is a serious avoidance pattern that you might be unaware of because it tends to be rare. The definition of a hypochondriac is a person who has an intense fear surrounding their health and whether or not they are okay. A slight physical pain can appear as a glaring sign that something is wrong with them. How is this relevant to grief, though? Your feelings of grief can transform from emotional hardship into mock pain. You might be 100% convinced that you are injured, sick, or dying as well. It is a scary situation to find yourself in, especially because you will not be able to see past the anxiety when you are in the moment.

Naturally, becoming a hypochondriac is consuming. Feeling that you are constantly in pain becomes a huge distraction that you will not be able to ignore. Pretty soon, it will take over your entire life. Because other people might not understand what you are going through, they will trivialize your pain or brush it off. This results in you feeling even more hurt and angry because what you are experiencing is real to you. These symptoms feel just as real as any other you have felt in your life.

You might begin to isolate yourself from certain people because they do not take your symptoms as seriously as you'd like. While you do not want the attention for the sake of being seen, you do want people to care about you as you are experiencing these various ailments. The worst part is that you feel like nothing you can do will change the way you feel. No matter what, you still feel the pain and anxiety of what might happen to you. It is unsettling, and it can happen quickly.

Grief does have certain physical symptoms associated with it, and these will become your reasoning for believing that you have something seriously wrong with you. Each time you feel an inkling of physical discomfort, you will focus on it and run with it. As you can see, this becomes a way to distract yourself because you are so worried about your health. It completely bypasses any need to think about the loss you have just endured or how to process it.

These symptoms should never be dismissed. If you are truly worried about the state of your health, seek professional help immediately. In cases like this, it is much better to be safe than sorry. Getting a professional opinion may or may not help with your hypochondria, but it will be a step in the right direction. Sometimes, all it takes is validation to start feeling better. When a doctor acknowledges that you are experiencing the symptoms you say you are, it might be easier for you to begin processing them and figuring out what to do next.

As mentioned, these are only some of the most common avoidance patterns during grief. You might experience others that have not been mentioned. The most important part is to pay attention to any patterns that arise. With the knowledge that you now have on healthy versus unhealthy coping behaviors, you should be able to distinguish when you are doing something considered out of character as you attempt to seek comfort during this difficult time. The sooner you get help for these behaviors, the sooner you will begin to feel better.

6

DEALING WITH ANGER WHILE GRIEVING

Feeling anger after you experience a loss is incredibly common. You already know that it happens to be a stage of grief, and it can appear at any time during the process. The level and type of anger you feel is going to be personal depending on how you lost the person. If your loved one died in a car accident, you might resent the other driver who was responsible for the wreck. If your loved one died of an illness in the hospital, you might have a hatred for the doctors that were caring for them at the time. There are so many ways that your anger can take over because it is so powerful.

In this chapter, you will learn how to face your anger and deal with it.

UNDERSTANDING ANGER

Your anger manifests from a place that is much deeper than you think. Yes, you are angry that your loved one is gone, but there is often a lot more to it than this. You might begin to question yourself as you feel an increase in anger as you are grieving. Where is this coming from? How can it be stopped? The best way to figure out a solution to your anger is by locating the source of it. Think deeper than the loss of your loved one. Being as specific as you can, narrow in on why you are so angry. Maybe you feel anger because you wish you could have done more to help this person when they were alive. Perhaps you had plans with this person that will no longer be accomplished.

There is usually always a deeper meaning, but it can take some time to access it. To better understand the anger you are feeling, ask yourself what it is about the situation that is hurting you or making you afraid. The answer is usually going to revolve around one or more of your basic survival needs. These are love, shelter, hunger, identity, affiliation, and security. When this person died, how many of your basic needs were threatened? You might be able to pinpoint just one, or you might feel that all of them have been affected. No matter how you are feeling, it is valid. Take note of the ways that this loss has changed your life.

After a death, there is usually a follow-up that comes with a set of changes. You might have to change your living situation, or the way that your friends and family interact with you might differ. Each change that occurs will naturally make you feel off-balance. The feeling of security that you once had is in the process of evolving, but you might mistake it for being completely taken away from you. Hence, the anger will start to set in. Nobody wants to feel discomfort willingly. Most of us experience a great deal of security because we have familiarity with our lives. Losing someone can make it seem like nothing will ever feel familiar again.

After you lose someone, venting can come naturally. This can serve as both a healthy and unhealthy coping mechanism to guide you through the stages of grief. By getting these strong emotions off your chest, you are probably going to feel better. There can be a lot of unresolved anger resting until you finally vent to someone you trust. Be cautious of who you choose to vent to and how much you are venting, though. In any relationship, there must be a mutual give-and-take. This means that if you are only seeking out the company of others when you want to vent your anger and frustration, they are probably going to start feeling taken for granted.

Though you are going through a big loss in your life, time passes, and feelings can be hurt. When you only reach out to people to vent without asking them how they are doing too, you create an imbalance in the relationship. This can happen with your friends, family members, and a significant other. No matter who this person is, you are close to them for a reason. Remain mindful that they have events and situations going on in their lives too. In fact, it might be helpful to stop and listen to what they'd like to vent about at times. When you hear about other problems that others face, you might feel less alone while you move through the process of grieving.

If there is a lot of unresolved anger, your venting sessions might be misinterpreted. Your anger will rise to the surface, and the person you are venting to might mistakenly believe you are angry with them for some reason. This can cause tension and strain on the relationship, pushing this person out of your life. When this happens, it is upsetting because you likely do not know why it is happening or how it got to this point. Try to reel in your anger as you are venting, being mindful of the fact that this person did not take your loved one away from you. There are probably many people in your life who would love to listen to you talk about anything for any length of time, so make sure you are appreciating them.

If you do lash out at a person you care about, you might want to tuck yourself away or avoid them because you do not want to have to face them. An apology is never something you will regret, so make sure you apologize when you are in the wrong.

You might realize that venting to your friends isn't going to satisfy your need to talk about the loss and why you are feeling so much anger. In this case, you should look into grief counseling. Many people are resistant to the idea at first because they are convinced that they do not need help. There is nothing wrong with getting help, though. The resources are available to you for a reason. If you can find a grief counselor and group meetings in your area, consider trying them out. Because they are in a more professional setting, you will get the chance to express your deepest emotions while also hearing about what strangers are going through. This can become an eye-opening experience that might end up helping you heal.

By listening to the struggles of others, it is easier to pinpoint what you still have to be grateful for. There are so many ways that you are still lucky and still destined to live a happy and full life, even if it does not seem this way right now. Anger can cloud your judgment, but it will not be like this forever. The sooner you become aware of your actions and start taking responsibility for them, the better you will feel.

Bring Awareness Back Into Your Life

After experiencing anger because of your loss, you might end up with feelings of guilt or unresolved thoughts. Try not to punish yourself for feeling this way because you can make a change for the better. Becoming more self-aware will rebalance your thoughts. If you want to apologize to those around you for acting out due to your emotions, do so, and they will likely understand and accept your apology. Work on bringing awareness into your life so that you do not lose control of your emotions when interacting with others.

The following are some tips on how to bring more awareness back into your life when you are ready to resolve your anger:

- **Ask for Feedback**: If you don't know if you are being too harsh, ask someone you trust. The answer may not be easy for you to accept, but you will hear an honest outside perspective. Acknowledging and accepting constructive criticism can help you to be the best version of yourself. Even while you are mourning, it is encouraged to work on your characteristics and flaws. There is never going to be a shortage of coping skills to learn and traits to adopt that will make you feel better.

- **Learn Something New**: Anger tends to appear more frequently when you are micromanaging other people and what they are doing. This type of coping mechanism can appear based on your need to feel like you have control. Because you could not control the loss of your loved one, you will try anything to feel like you are regaining this control.

By teaching yourself something new, whether it be a new word each day or a new hobby, you can healthily feel like you are in control again.

- **Identify Inaccurate Thoughts**: When you are acting out of anger, you are likely to have irrational thoughts. These are identifiable based on their lack of supporting details. For example, if you feel that all of your friends dislike you now because you have been sad due to your loss, give yourself some reasons as to why this is not true. You might discover that your friends still check on you, want to spend time with you, and want to make sure that you heal from your loss. All of these signs point to a different conclusion, and it is important to be aware of this. Your mind can be your worst nightmare if you let these irrational thoughts take over. It can trigger anger inside of you that does not need to exist in the first place.

- **Clarify Your Values**: Your entire life has just changed because of this loss, and it is okay to admit that you feel this in a big way. When you no longer know what to focus on, it is common to experience anger and frustration. You can get back to your true self by reidentifying the things that matter most, like your current values. These values are personal, and you do not have to share them with anybody if you are uncomfortable. Simply restate your values to yourself to give you an idea of who you are as a person. Having this reassurance will make you feel confident and secure again.

- **Pay Attention to Triggers in Others**: You might feel like you are okay with who you are as a person, but it is other people that you find yourself frustrated with. This anger still stems from a trigger. Try to identify what triggers you in the behavior of other people. It is likely that their behavior either reminds you of yourself or your flaws; this is why it is bothering you so much. You might find that you are taking your anger out on others when, in reality, you are simply angry at yourself because you can identify with their weaknesses.

- **Meditate on Angry Thoughts**: When you feel like you can no longer cope with your anger or discuss it, meditate on it. Sit down in a quiet room with these thoughts, allowing them to manifest in the way that they need to. This will become an enlightening process for you, likely to highlight the true root of your problem. When you give yourself some solitary moments of thinking, you'll be surprised by what comes up.

ANGER CAN BE GOOD

Every negative emotion comes with a silver lining. There are some instances where your anger can be a positive thing. Some believe anger is an essential part of the grieving process. Without experiencing it, you might not fully heal.

There is not necessarily a "right" way to get angry, but there are ways to tell when the anger is healthy and improving your state of being. You can use your anger as a tool to help you get through your hardships. When you learn how to recognize and redirect it, you are reclaiming your power. To fully experience the best your anger has to offer, you need to be honest with yourself. When you are feeling angry, do not deny or stifle the feeling. Accept it because you must accept it before you can understand it.

Once you have learned how to recognize these moments, do not take immediate action. You need to see how the feeling is going to manifest. If you rush to stop it, you might be hindering yourself. Work with the feeling until it leads you to some point of action. The action is either going to be destructive, healthy, or neutral. If it is harmful to you or those around you, then you can intervene. When you feel it for a healthy or neutral reason, it is best to simply let the anger play out. Let all of the emotions go, willingly releasing them by using coping mechanisms you have learned.

The better you become at this self-identification process, the better you can communicate with others when you are feeling bad. If you know that you are angry and it is not the other person's fault, stating that you feel angry or upset can help to ease some of the tension that is building. You can tell them that it is not their fault but still warn them of the fact that you feel this way. This provides your loved ones with insight. They might not have known that you were feeling this way, but hearing it directly from you will offer them clarity.

You might not be willing to accept their kind words or gestures of help right now, and this is okay. If you feel that your loved ones are being too involved or overbearing when you are angry, communicate with them. Tell them that you would prefer to work through the issues alone but that you appreciate the support. This is a clear and concise way to express yourself without feeling like you are being backed into a corner. Having this newfound clarity should resolve a lot of the anger that might be unintentionally taken out on those who are trying to help you. Anyone who loves and respects you will be willing to back off as long as you are not in danger.

With your defensiveness at bay, your mind will feel clearer to seek solutions. This experience will show you that your anger can lead to a positive outcome. The more that you experience this, the less you will feel the need to suppress your anger. It can still be okay, even on the days when you feel the rage inside. You are going to have your ups and downs, but this is just a part of the entire grieving process, as you know. Work with these moments, being patient with yourself every step of the way. It may help to imagine that your best friend or most cherished loved one was going through the same thing. How would you treat them? When you can apply this same kindness to yourself, you will start to feel better.

What this experience all comes down to is, once again, realizing what you can and cannot control. If you are angry over something that cannot be changed, you need to realize that there is no traveling backward in time. You need to keep looking ahead, but that does not mean you cannot make changes right now that will improve the present. When you live in the moment, you will start to seek better solutions. You can use the anger that you feel like a passion to apply these changes in your life. Let it motivate you and guide you along the way. Working with your anger is just like working with any other emotion you feel. The more familiar you become with its patterns, the better you will become at comforting yourself.

Slow down when you begin to feel the anger rising in your chest. Acting on your anger can often result in an expedited feeling that will then lead to that out-of-control type of response. Take a few deep breaths when you start feeling overwhelmed; it helps more than you think. Realize that, more often than not, you are not being pressured or timed regarding your decision-making. You can take the time to work through your anger before you decide how you want to react. The rash decisions you make are the ones that you usually regret. We have all said things out of anger that we wish we hadn't, and these moments could have probably been avoided if we had just taken a moment to slow down.

Even when someone is standing in front of you and waiting for a response, you do not need to jump right in. Explain that you need a minute, and emotionally remove yourself from the situation. Even pausing for a short amount of time can help you to figure out what you need to say or do next. It is also okay if you do not know what must be done. Be honest with that person, and explain to them if you need more time to think or to be with your thoughts. Everyone heals at a different rate, and you do not need to feel guilty that you cannot instantly make decisions when you are angry. It takes a lot of patience and self-control to harness your emotions until you can think clearly. This skill will help you out in many ways throughout your life.

To better help yourself recognize when you need to stop, pause, or slow down, you can use this "speed limit" guide to help:

90 MPH	Explosive, violent
85 MPH	Fuming, outraged
80 MPH	Infuriated, enraged
75 MPH	Irate, exasperated
70 MPH	Bitter, indignant
65 MPH	Pissed off
60 MPH	Mad, angry
55 MPH	Agitated, perturbed
50 MPH	Annoyed, frustrated
45 MPH	Displeased, ruffled
40 MPH	Peaceful, tranquil

When using this guide, check in with yourself often. After you locate the emotions you are feeling, you can apply a "speed" to your level of anger. Next, you must decide what your speed limit is. What speed will you reach that requires some kind of intervention? Most people can handle minor annoyances and frustration, but there is no standard speed limit, especially when you are grieving. Keep in mind that your speed limit can also change as you heal. Once it is set, you can monitor your emotions, ensuring you are staying within this self-declared comfort zone.

Make a plan for what you will do if you start speeding. The most logical thing to do in any case is to slow down. By taking a moment to yourself to breathe or by engaging in a healthy coping behavior, you should be able to slow down your rate of anger. Using this chart can become a helpful way for you to manage your anger any time it surfaces.

You can also use visualization to help enforce your speed limit. Imagine that you are being pulled over when you notice that you are speeding. How fast were you going? Think about this as a warning that you are giving to yourself. Without punishing yourself for speeding, take this warning to heart, and consider what you can do to slow down and take better care of yourself. If you find yourself speeding again, think about getting pulled over one more time. In this case, you might need to make an active change to prevent yourself from going over the speed limit.

Removing yourself from your current environment can be a helpful way to manage your anger. If you are stewing in your negative feelings for a long time, these feelings are going to linger where you are. Going on a walk around the block can help tremendously, for example, because you are encouraging yourself to get out and experience a change in the atmosphere. You are going to be sensitive to other energy around you when you are dealing with anger. Pick up on the positive energy that you notice, using it as fuel to motivate you to head in a more positive direction. Spending time with people who are uplifting or spending time in nature are two ways that you can get the energetic recharge that you are craving.

Many people struggle with managing their anger, even before they lose a loved one. It is such a powerful emotion, and it might seem like you have no choice but to give in. Now, you are equipped with tools that you can use to fight back. Do not give in the instant that you feel your anger approaching. Understand it and realize that it is happening. Acknowledge it just as you would with your happiness and joy. This is how you are going to use it in a positive and healthy way.

The journey won't always be easy, but it will be worth it.

HOW TO COPE

You will learn which coping skills work best for your anger during this time. It is a good idea to start journaling so you can keep track of when you usually feel angry and why. Write down how you are feeling each day to spot any patterns in your behavior. This is going to help you cope well and adjust to this stage of grief that you must work through. Write down all of the coping mechanisms you try as well. Just because one does not seem to work on certain triggers does not mean it won't work on others. Anger can evolve, just like any other emotion. Being mindful of this, the following are some coping mechanisms to give you ideas of the kinds of behaviors you can try that might end up being successful for you.

Count Down

The next time you feel your anger rising, start counting. You can count down from 100 until you feel like your anger is subsiding. This seems like a simple coping mechanism because it is. It provides your brain with just enough of a distraction to redirect your thoughts. You might end up realizing that you aren't as angry about the situation as you thought you were. Once you feel like your anger is manageable, you can stop counting to regroup. Consider what can be done and what your end goal is. This will promote a focus on positive coping mechanisms.

Walk

Whether you go outdoors or into the next room, walking will provide you with a small dose of endorphins. These are the happy chemicals that result from participating in physical activity. Walk around until you can feel your anger subsiding. While this is not going to cure the anger that you feel or the situation you are experiencing, it will lessen the severity of it. This will result in a more manageable feeling that will allow you to regain control of your behaviors.

Relax Your Muscles

Because anger is an emotion, you might not even think that it can create physical ailments. But holding a lot of tension inside brings you symptoms such as muscle soreness, stomach pain, and headaches. Taking a long, hot bath can help to relax your muscles when you are angry. Even simply lying down for a few moments and working on muscle isolations can improve your state of mind. To do this, close your eyes and imagine that you are relaxing your body from the tips of your toes to the top of your head. Work your way up until you have fully relaxed all of your muscles.

Recite a Mantra

Using a mantra is like relying on a certain word or phrase to inspire you throughout the day. Your mantra can be anything that uplifts you. "I will get through this" is an example of something general and applicable to almost every situation. When you are feeling angry and like you are about to reach your breaking point, breathe and recite your mantra in your head. If possible, recite it out loud to yourself in the mirror. The goal is to say it enough that you convince yourself of the positive affirmation you are repeating.

Mentally Escape

Using visualization to leave your situation for a moment can help the anger subside. Close your eyes and imagine the most relaxing place you can think of. This place might be somewhere you've been before or it might only exist in your mind. No matter where you go, tell yourself that your anger cannot follow you here; this is a safe space. Think about what the area looks and sounds like. Are there other people with you or are you there by yourself? Try to think about all of the smallest details as they will start to add up and bring positivity into your life.

Play Some Music

The power of music can be healing. When you notice that your mood is declining, play your favorite songs. It helps to have a playlist handy for when these moments occur. By hearing the familiar and welcoming tunes, you are naturally going to lighten up. The power of music can be transformative, often taking you to different places mentally. Allow yourself to get lost in each song, listening to the beat, the instruments, and the lyrics. If you feel compelled, you can even dance as you feel each tune.

Stop Talking

Hearing your own words being projected can often trigger your anger. You are already feeling frustrated, so stop trying to over-explain yourself or defend your feelings. Instead, take the time to do the opposite.

Oftentimes, the source of your anger will make its appearance during this silence. Welcome it if this happens. The silence can be scary sometimes, but you can learn to use it as a tool to get to the bottom of your negativity.

Take Action

Even if you are not working directly on solving the problem, you can harness your anger in other ways. Use it to stir up the passionate side of you. If there is a cause that you can contribute to, do so. This can make you feel productive and will be a useful way to unleash this energy. When you feel that your contributions matter, you are going to be momentarily satisfied. This temporary relief from your anger can help you to calm down and move forward.

Select an Immediate Solution

You already know that there are many things you can do to take action when you are experiencing anger. Out of all of the solutions you come up with, rank them from the most immediate to the most time-consuming. When you can pick a solution that provides you with immediate relief, you are going to feel a lot better. Not to be confused with instant gratification, this solution for your anger should still revolve around healthy coping mechanisms and lasting positive effects.

Picture a Stop Sign

This is another coping skill that seems trivial, but it can help you by being a direct reminder. As you feel yourself approaching the edge of your anger, imagine a big stop sign in front of you. Picture it clearly, red with bold font. Use this as a chance to take caution before you reach an explosive level of anger. Sometimes, you need to provide yourself with the warning signs before your mind is trained to do so on its own. You need to condition yourself to learn that there are consequences for making rash decisions.

Change Your Routine

Aspects of your routine can lead to annoyance and frustration. From the traffic that you encounter on your drive to work to the other inconveniences you face, your anger can reach its tipping point when you never make any changes to your routine. After a loss, changing your routine can feel refreshing. Drive a different route, and make your life easier during this time. This will help with your anger, and it can also help to make life feel less stressful.

Laugh

You might feel like you don't have many reasons to laugh nowadays, but the cliché is true; laughter can feel like the best medicine when you are down. If nothing comical is making you laugh, try laughing at nothing. This might feel odd, but it is going to release happy chemicals in your brain that will promote the state of your well-being. You might end up really laughing because you feel funny for making yourself laugh. Try to watch funny movies or listen to amusing stories.

During this time, you want to promote as much uplifting energy in your life as you can.

Practice Gratitude

The next time you feel like you are about to lash out in anger, try stopping and writing down three things that you are grateful for. They can be people, traits, objects, or anything that reminds you that you are still lucky. Putting things into perspective like this will teach you that there is still so much in your life to appreciate. When you lose someone you love, it can feel like life isn't worth living anymore. You need to give yourself consistent reminders that there are always going to be silver linings, as long as you seek them.

Set a Timer

Whenever you are feeling an urge to act on your anger, set a timer for five minutes. Before you respond based on how you are feeling, allow this time to pass without taking any action. You don't have to think about anything in particular, but pay attention to the way you are feeling. You'd be surprised how much these feelings can change if you simply allow some time and space between your thoughts and actions. Evaluate if you still want to act out in the way that you originally did once the timer goes off. This exercise will serve as a reminder that you need to be more patient with yourself to healthily process what you are feeling.

Write a Letter

When somebody triggers your anger, you cannot always speak your mind at the moment. Instead, write everything down in a letter to said person. Without censoring yourself, write down all of the things that are bothering you and why. Pretend that you are saying them directly to the person you feel angry with. After you are finished, read the letter. Feel the anger leaving your mind and body as it transfers onto the page. Make a point to keep reading what you have written until you feel like the anger has left you. Then, get rid of the letter. You can throw it away, rip it up, burn it, or do anything that feels good to you. This is a symbolic way to get your negativity out, and it allows you to vent about what you are going through without causing any conflict or tension.

Find Freedom

Sometimes, you are going to feel angry, yet you are going to be the one who is in the wrong. Understand that it is never beneath you to apologize when you make a mistake. Find freedom in the process of taking accountability for your actions. Nobody is perfect, yourself included. Having the power to recognize that you have made a mistake and that you care about another person's feelings enough to apologize is a great trait to maintain. Feel proud of yourself for doing the right thing and allowing the anger to be set free through your apology.

These are only some of the ways that you can practice to cope with your anger. As you explore them, you will find other ways that might end up working better for you. Anger is a personal emotion as not everyone is triggered by the same events and situations. Also, not everyone is experiencing a loss like you are. Be mindful of the entire process, even the parts that are difficult to manage. Through these healthy expressions of anger, you will slowly release it from your mind and body. Remind yourself that this is only one of the stages of grief that you must get through. Eventually, the way you feel is going to evolve.

It might shock you how much your temper flares up during this time, but try not to be so hard on yourself; you are not the same version of yourself you once were. Loss is traumatic, and trauma can change people. While you might never be the same version of yourself as you once were, you can certainly find your way back to your core values.

Imagine what the most important things in your life are right now. Even if you can only think of one or two of them, this gives you an excellent foundation to live your life. Make what is important to you a priority. This means setting new goals and striving to be better for whatever it is that you value. You might feel lost and confused right now, but that moment of clarity will come for you.

7

HOW TO USE THE WIM HOF METHOD TO DEAL WITH GRIEF

W im Hof has completed some impressive accomplishments in his lifetime. He is a Dutch athlete and a 26-time world record holder at 61 years old. Hof claims that he can control his nervous system with his own will thanks to his special training model. The model allows him to withstand both physical and mental extremes, and others who follow it can control their nervous systems as well. The Wim Hof Method mainly consists of breathing exercises and exposure to the elements that are thought to help you reclaim more conscious control than you have ever had before.

But how does this relate to dealing with grief? Well, grief tends to do the opposite; it makes you lose consciousness and touch with reality as you are sucked into your emotions. As we discussed before, being aware of how you feel can help you when you are stuck in your grief.

Unfortunately, Hof himself is familiar with grief. In 1995, he lost his wife to suicide, leaving him to raise their four children on his own. An unimaginable hardship, he struggled to work through the stages of grief and balance the many responsibilities placed on his shoulders. He knew that he had to become mentally stronger if he was going to survive, not only for his sake but to honor his wife and to raise their children.

This need to be strong led Hof to create his Wim Hof Method. While it is something unconventional that you probably never imagined trying before, it has been beneficial in his own life and with the ailments that he has faced while grieving.

While reading about this method, remain mindful of the fact that this all stemmed from the hardship of loss. Just as you are struggling right now, Hof also experienced his own struggle. You are not alone when you are feeling at your absolute lowest point. Hof reached this point during his period of grief, but he was able to overcome it through a lot of self-discipline. This is the only way that you are going to be able to rewire your brain and heal yourself, or so Hof believes.

In this chapter, the method will be expanded to give you a clear understanding of what it takes to gain complete control of your nervous system. In turn, this will help you cope with your grief in a proactive way. While the method might feel intense to you, there are ways to safely transition into it to get your mind and body used to these changes.

Although the Wim Hof Method is not a guaranteed way to free you from the constructs of your grief, it will allow you to make a solid attempt. As you are searching for answers and feeling confused during your grief, committing yourself to something immersive might be exactly what it takes to give yourself an extra boost of strength.

THREE BASIC PRINCIPLES

The Wim Hof Method consists of three different parts: controlled hyperventilation, exhalation, and retention. This can sound overwhelming at first, but these principles are broken down into steps to allow you to achieve them without much difficulty. You will also become better at them as you train, much like an athlete improves their performance.

As an athlete, Wim Hof was used to rigorous training and goal-setting, so he incorporated these values into his method. He understands that you are not going to simply feel better overnight after you use this method one time. You need to be consistent with it, and you need to practice if you want to see an improvement.

Let's start with hyperventilation, which is when you breathe more rapidly than normal.

At first, the idea of hyperventilation sounds negative. You likely associate it with panic and feeling uneasy. Going through grief, there are likely moments when you experience it in a negative way. A lot of people hyperventilate when they first find out the terrible news that they have lost a loved one because it is a programmed response that happens when your brain does not know how to process the information it has received. Part of the Wim Hof Method is taking back the power from the things that make you powerless, and your breathing is one of them. It is no secret that your breath can be controlled. This has been practiced since ancient times in yoga. By controlling your breathing, you are regulating your mind and body.

To begin the Wim Hof Method, use the following steps:

1. Take 30 powerful breaths in a row, inhaling deeply to fill the lungs.
2. Passively release the air from your lungs, allowing it to escape naturally. After you have released it, hold your breath for 1 to 3 minutes or as long as you can.
3. Take another deep inhale and hold for 15 to 20 seconds before releasing the breath.

As you repeat this exhalation process, you should begin to feel a slight tingling in your arms and legs. This is a sign that you are doing it correctly. Feeling slightly lightheaded is also normal. You must be careful as you begin to practice controlled hyperventilation because it can be dangerous to disrupt your breathing too consistently. You must always practice this in a seated, controlled position. Never hyperventilate while you are in the bathtub or anywhere where you might fall and get injured.

When you first start the Wim Hof Method, you should not exceed 30 inhalations during a single session. This is going to be a lot on the average person's lungs. The idea is to give yourself a challenge but to avoid being detrimental to your mind and body. Once you have more experience, you might be able to withstand 60 inhalations, but your goal should not be to increase this number. Instead, focus on getting yourself to the point of a steady rhythm. After this, you can move on to the next step, which is exhalation. You will take a final inhalation as you are hyperventilating, and then you will focus on regulating your breath once more.

Your cycles are now complete, and it is time to fully exhale. As you do, let the air escape slowly and in a controlled fashion. This time, you are going to empty your lungs to breathe normally again. Imagine your entire body being revitalized now.

By completing these first two steps, you have changed the way that you are breathing in its entirety. The final step is retention. You are going to feel a strong urge to inhale once you complete your long exhalation. As soon as this happens and your lungs are empty, allow yourself to inhale deeply and hold this breath for 15 to 20 seconds. The goal here is not to make your breathing jagged again but instead to regulate it.

At this point, you might experience a head rush. Continue to remain seated for a few minutes after you complete this breathing exercise. If you feel the need, you can repeat the retention step up to three times. Be cautious of your lightheadedness.

Immediately after you finish the three basic steps, try getting into a cold shower. It should not feel as cold or jarring to you as it normally does, and this is because you have reset your nervous system. You might even feel like the water is warm and comfortable! It is incredible what you can do if you simply put your mind to it.

Wim Hof also encourages you to try to work out after you feel that you have regained your breath. The physical activity should not feel as strenuous as it normally does.

I do my breathe work in the shower and as soon as I'm finished, I crank the shower to cold and focus on my breathing. Be mindful that I have been doing this for a while and I'm able to stand while I do it. If you're new you may want to slowly expose yourself to cold water therapy by finishing your shower with a 15-30 second cold portion.

BENEFITS

The breathing exercise from the Wim Hof Method comes with several advantages. Because you are revitalizing the way you breathe, you are almost going to feel a surge in power. This type of breathing releases a big amount of energy, which is why you feel so recharged after completing it. It influences your nervous system and changes various physiological responses.

One of the biggest benefits is what the Wim Hof Method will do for your stress levels. When you practice the breathing exercise, you trigger what is known as the short stress response. This means that you will feel more resilient to the stressors that appear in your daily life.

You are probably familiar with the days where every stressor feels like it can break you down. This becomes especially true as you experience stress while grieving. Even the smallest inconvenience can feel like the end of the world. By practicing the Wim Hof Method, you are giving yourself more strength and protection against these stressors. The calmness and resilience that you feel will encourage you to believe that things will be okay again. This is important because the loss you are going through tends to make it seem like your sense of what is normal has been shattered.

Stress is not only detrimental to your mental health; it can also destroy your physical well-being. When you constantly live under the weight of your stressors, your body feels tired and worn down. You might not feel like you have enough energy to complete your normal tasks, which can lead to feelings of helplessness. As you know, this can often become a precursor to serious mental illnesses such as depression. Stress is not something that you should force yourself to live with. It is an ailment that can make any loss seem more painful and exaggerated, but you can lessen its effects when you control your breathing.

Having more control is a feeling that nearly every human craves. The things that happen to us in life are often going to be outside of our control, especially negative things. This is why our programmed responses are so important. As you practice the breathing exercise that Wim Hof provides, you are restoring your faith in your ability to control your responses. This is going to build you up and get you through even your hardest moments. Imagine what Wim Hof went through as he simultaneously grieved his lost wife and had to continue to raise their children. This unimaginable pain is something that you can probably relate to the loss of your loved one.

Another benefit of the Wim Hof Method is the ability to quickly recover from physical activity. Even if you are not running marathons and working out daily, your body is naturally going to feel more tired when you are grieving. Simple tasks will wear you out, but regulating your nervous system can help to rebalance the way you feel. In turn, this also impacts your ability to sleep; you will find it easier to fall asleep and will be able to get restful sleep. If you have been struggling with this since the loss, you will find a lot of relief. Getting a good night's sleep can change your entire outlook on your day ahead.

You might also discover that your creative brain has experienced a surge in activity. While creativity is not necessary during mourning, it can help you as a healthy coping mechanism. Being able to think outside of the box and to express yourself with creativity gives you something else to focus on other than the loss you have experienced. Take advantage of this benefit by attempting to do something creative on a regular basis. You can paint, draw, write, dance, sing, or do anything that feels good to you. This will become an uplifting part of your routine, and you will find it helpful in regulating your mood and emotions.

One of the best benefits of the Wim Hof Method is enhanced mental clarity. Grief puts you through a lot of uncertainty and doubt. You might be stuck on the idea that you don't know how to go on in life without your loved one or that you do not want to, but with a restored sense of clarity, you will find your way back to your core values. Your life will have meaning once again, and you might even feel motivated to create new goals for yourself. Starting small is not a bad thing. Even if you can only manage to work on one goal at a time, this is a step in the right direction. It will give you a sense of purpose and guidance that you need during this time.

Lastly, an interesting benefit of the Wim Hof Method is its ability to lower your symptoms and risk factors for certain diseases, such as arthritis, Parkinson's, asthma, and several autoimmune disorders. As we age and experience stress, the risk factors for many of these diseases increase. You can use the Wim Hof Method as a preventative measure against them. The last thing that you need is to fall ill or to struggle even more during this time. After all, part of the grieving process includes taking care of yourself as you simultaneously go through each stage.

SCIENCE

To better understand the Wim Hof Method and why it can provide you with all of the above benefits, it is essential to understand the science behind it. By breaking this down, you will have a clear idea of what is going on inside of your mind and body as you complete the breathing exercise.

Most people are familiar with the basic concept of why breathing deeply is so great for you. When we breathe, oxygen is inhaled, and carbon dioxide is exhaled. When carbon dioxide is in your system, it reacts with water to create carbonic acid. When your blood is more acidic, your ability to breathe slowly and regularly is impacted. You will find the need to take sharper, jagged breaths. Panic is more likely to happen as well. Overall, acidic blood means less stability as you cycle through your negative emotions.

The Wim Hof Method lowers your carbon dioxide levels since you are exhaling more deeply. This creates a more blanched pH level in your blood, which means that it is alkaline. According to researchers at Radboud University Medical Center, this is why you tend to experience the tingling in your limbs as you perform the Wim Hof Method

(Sinicki 2018). Your body goes into a state of "intermittent respiratory alkalosis," meaning your blood is alkaline as you control your hyperventilation. Making your blood more alkaline also means that you are preventing your body from properly using its oxygen stores. This can sound dangerous, but it prompts your body to "recycle" the oxygen instead of becoming dependent on new oxygen to breathe properly.

When you are holding your inhalation in the second step of the Wim Hof Method, the recycling process takes place. Without it, you would likely become too lightheaded and end up passing out. The carbon dioxide is recycled just enough when you hold your breath for the short period that you can take it in. This is why practicing more inhalations of controlled hyperventilation is never the goal. It becomes dangerous easily, and you do not want to overdo it.

Adrenaline

During the process of completing the Wim Hof Method, your body starts to create adrenaline. This is what is responsible for your fight-or-flight response and the feeling of wanting to take a deep breath. Part of this feeling is triggered by panic and your body's desire to breathe normally, but there is another part that is thought to be triggered by the vagus nerve. This is the longest of your cranial nerves, and its purpose is to monitor your bodily functions and processes. So, while your body might be entering its fight-or-flight response because the adrenaline has kicked in, it will also begin to be regulated by the vagus nerve. This nerve responds to many triggers, such as temperature, oxygen levels, the inner workings of your gut, and more.

Calm vs. Panicked

You might be wondering why it isn't more beneficial to just breathe deeply and calmly like in yoga and martial arts. When you breathe this way, your body is telling the parasympathetic nervous system that all is well. This lowers your heart rate and tells your body that it is okay to slow down and pay less attention to what is going on. With faster, panicked breathing, you experience hyper-focus and concentration. Since the parasympathetic nervous system is on alert that something might not be okay, it gives you a boost of energy to get through whatever it is that you are trying to overcome.

Some studies show it is healthy to stimulate the vagus nerve in this way when dealing with certain mental illnesses. Because grief can put you in such a downward spiral pattern, it is thought that you do not need to calm down to feel better. You need to completely change the way your body is operating, and giving yourself this sudden boost of energy can do just that.

Long-Term Effects

In simple terms, it has already been stated that you are temporarily making your blood more alkaline as you complete the Wim Hof Method, but what does this mean for the long-term? If you decide you'd like to regularly use this method to trigger responses in your body and receive benefits, you are also going to benefit from the production of more red blood cells. When your oxygen levels are reduced, EPO is secreted. EPO, or erythropoietin, is a hormone that is essential to the production of your red blood cells. If you are regularly reducing your oxygen levels, the EPO is going to spread throughout your body more frequently.

This means that you are also going to experience the ability to perform tasks that require more endurance. While you might not have any desire to become a professional athlete like Wim Hof, you already know how difficult average tasks feel as you are going through the hardship of your loss. Any boost in endurance is going to feel like some much-needed assistance, no matter what stage of grief you are in. This is thought to have a similar effect to high-altitude training. When athletes need to build their endurance, they train in places that have a higher altitude because it takes more energy to complete the same tasks. At a higher altitude, it becomes harder to breathe because the oxygen levels change.

Next, you must take into account the other part of the method—cold exposure. Your body is exposed to something normally shocking, but it can withstand the effects. In the long-term, this type of exposure is thought to train your immune system to become stronger. According to a study by the *European Journal of Applied Physiology and Occupational Physiology*, because of this exposure, the body learned how to raise lymphocytes, which are white blood cells that are found in the vertebrate immune system (Sinicki 2018). These cells are essential to your immune system.

Most people are under the misconception that exposure to the cold will make them sick. You probably grew up hearing from your parents to wear a jacket to avoid catching a cold. The reason why you end up getting sick after exposure to the cold is that you were already at risk. Since the cold suppresses your immune system, you become more vulnerable. With the ability to control your immune system and to make it stronger, you can experience colder elements without falling ill. When you repeatedly challenge your immune system by practicing the Wim Hof Method, it will continue to become stronger.

Key Scientific Studies

Below is a collection of additional studies done on the Wim Hof Method that back its benefits. Through this research, you will be able to better understand exactly what your body is going through and why it is seen as a positive change.

Radboud University, The Netherlands (2014)

- Focused on testing a larger group in the same way that they first tested Wim Hof back in 2011
- 12 practitioners of the Wim Hof Method were injected with endotoxin
- Results were similar to Wim Hof's—they were able to control their parasympathetic nervous system and boost their immune response
- Anti-inflammatory protection was 200%+ higher
- Conditions associated with inflammation, such as autoimmune disorders, were thought to see benefits if the upkeep of the method were to take place

Wayne State University, Michigan, United States (2018)

- The "Brain Over Body" study

- Focused on understanding brain function that allows Wim Hof to withstand extremely cold temperatures
- Wim Hof wore a temperature control suit and was placed in an MRI machine and a PET scan machine
- Results revealed his brain activated pain suppression

CONNECTION TO GRIEF

You have experienced sadness many times before, but the intensity of the sadness that your grief brings can feel different. In most cases of sadness, you can navigate your way through without much disruption to your routines and schedule.

However, because loss is so powerful, personal, and outside of your control, the sadness is going to feel a lot worse. You already know that this sadness can develop into clinical depression if left untreated. The longer that you feel sad, the more you are at risk of becoming clinically depressed. This is why some type of intervention becomes necessary. Without any treatment, you are left to struggle with your feelings of sadness on your own.

There are ways that the scientific benefits of the Wim Hof Method can help your sadness and depression. When you become clinically depressed, your blood becomes more inflamed. These higher amounts of inflammation are typically found in those who are struggling with chronic depression. Since the Wim Hof Method has been proven to lower these rates of inflammation in your body, it is going to help you overcome your sadness and depression from the inside out. On a physical level, there isn't much else that you can do to change your inflammation levels. This is what makes the method so powerful.

Wim Hof is a believer in holistic ways of healing, and the more natural the better. Besides going to therapy and seeking help this way, you can also work on taking certain actions at home that will allow your life to feel more carefree. These activities help you to fight the negative thoughts from the source as they are mind-focused. You will ultimately be able to overcome your sadness once you get to the root cause of your negativity.

While there are several natural healing options out there, below are some of the ones I recommend.

Meditation

There are tens of thousands of studies on meditation and how it is impactful when it comes to treating sadness and depression. The art of meditation has been practiced since ancient times, and it continues to be a favorite activity that is sought out by those who wish to take a holistic approach to healing.

There is no right or wrong way to meditate. The idea is that you must focus your mind on something positive and peaceful to prevent negative or sad thoughts from taking over. In some ways, the Wim Hof Method is like meditation because you are putting intense focus on your breathing.

To practice meditation in a more traditional sense, you have a few options. You can go to a meditation class that is led by a teacher, you can find a guided meditation online, or you can lead yourself through a self-guided session. Depending on your level of experience with meditation and your overall comfort, your choice will vary. Remember, any of these forms of meditation are going to be beneficial to you. As long as you have a private area to meditate that is quiet and peaceful, you will be able to make the most of your session.

When you are left alone with only your thoughts, which happens during meditation, it is unsurprising that the negative ones try to surface the fastest. Instead of suppressing these thoughts, give them the chance to form and acknowledge them. Do not hold on to them or try to fix them at the moment; instead, imagine that they are floating away on a running current of a river. As you envision each negative or sad thought being washed along the river, think about how this is making room for new thoughts. With time, the negative ones will eventually subside.

When you meditate, you can keep a mantra or a positive affirmation in mind. This is your intention that you are putting into your meditation session. Think of it as what you hope to achieve. A good starting point is peace or clarity. Grief can make you feel like you have lost both, so seeking more is going to benefit you at this point in your life. Much like any form of healing, you cannot expect to feel 100% better after you meditate once, but practice will make a difference. The idea is that you can make meditation a bigger part of your life, practicing it often. Just as there is no correct way to meditate, there is also no limit on how much you can meditate.

Most people choose to meditate either first thing in the morning or before bed. Usually, your mind is going to be clearest when you first wake up, so making time for meditation will get your day started on a positive note. Alternatively, meditating before bed becomes a great way to clear your mind, which will allow you to sleep better. You can even do both if you have the time and energy for it.

Physical Activity

Engaging in any type of physical activity while you are grieving is highly encouraged. Creating more endorphins in your brain allows you to feel happier. Working out or moving is probably one of the last things that you feel like doing as you are going through your grief, but getting past the initial resistance to it can help you. Commit to doing at least two to three different types of physical activity each week. These activities do not have to be complex or strenuous. Even just taking a walk around your neighborhood can be enough to release these endorphins and make you feel a lot better.

As an athlete, Wim Hof relied on endorphins to get him through his grief. While you don't need to be a super athlete like Wim Hof, being able to focus on something productive is going to benefit you. Knowing that doing something physical is not only healthy for you but can also present you with a set of goals can prove a much-needed sense of relief.

The following are some forms of physical activity that you can partake in when you feel like you need to get up and moving:

- Dancing
- Stretching
- Jogging
- Weight-lifting

- Doing chores
- Preparing meals
- Walking around your house

Do whatever you feel comfortable with, and remember that you might have to build up your will to complete these tasks in the beginning. Even if you can only manage to get up and walk around your room one time, this is still an improvement. You will get your legs moving and begin to feel a slight rush of endorphins in your brain.

Partaking in physical activities also promotes the growth of new brain cells. As they form, you will find that you can get a better night's sleep. This is essential for someone who is going through the grieving process. You will also feel an increase in your self-esteem, which has naturally suffered a blow since you have been dealing with so much uncertainty in your life during this time.

A great way to enhance this process is to perform your physical activity outside in the sunshine if possible. The added benefits that you get from receiving natural vitamin D will make you feel even happier. We all need vitamin D to live healthy lives, so making sure that you are getting enough of it during this time is more important than ever. Monitor the way you feel when you perform your physical activity indoors versus outdoors in the sunlight. You are guaranteed to feel a difference when you are done.

Support

It becomes so easy to withdraw from everyone in your life when you are experiencing the hardship of grief. Maybe you do not want to explain to other people how you are feeling, or maybe you do not want to talk about your loss any longer. No matter the cause, it becomes hard to think about spending time around other people, even if they have your best intentions in mind.

To make the idea of socializing less overwhelming, remind yourself that you do not have to socialize with everyone who wants to see you. As you are working through your feelings, realize that you can decide who you'd like to spend your time around. It is always a good idea to be around someone you already felt comfortable with before because this takes away a lot of the pressure of socialization. Since this person already knows you well, there will be less of a need to explain yourself or the way you are feeling. You will be able to simply spend time with them and feed off of their energy.

The people you choose to be close to during this time must be providing you with nothing but uplifting energy. You do not need any more bad energy right now, and if someone makes you feel this way, it is not selfish to temporarily distance yourself from them until you are feeling better. This is a process, and it will have many ups and downs. The people in your life, no matter how close you are, might not always know what you want or need during this period of healing. This is why it helps you express yourself as best as you can. Tell others what they can do for you as they are probably already there and willing to help you get through this.

Most people tend to feel selfish when they must ask for what they need, but this is not the case; knowing what you need to feel better only showcases your strength. It is not wrong for you to ask for love and support right now because you need it more than ever. Be kind to yourself, just as the people in your life are being kind to you. Listen to them talk about their lives and struggles. This change in conversation might help you by showing you different perspectives and other ways of life. It is a reminder that you are not alone in the fact that you are having a hard time, and other people are going through their version of the human experience.

Diet

What you eat matters because it becomes the fuel that keeps you going. When you are feeling sad and stressed, you might want to reach for your comfort foods. For most people, this means a lot of processed foods and sugars. Most of the time, junk food is considered a comfort food because it is convenient and artificially processed to taste good. Treating yourself to these things every once in a while is okay, but you need to make sure that you are maintaining a balanced diet overall. Seek out foods that are high in vitamins and nutrients to protect your mind and body. These are some essentials that you should be including in your diet during this time:

- Nuts
- Legumes
- Whole grains
- Dark leafy greens
- Eggs
- Salmon
- Dark chocolate
- Asparagus
- Broccoli

- Blueberries
- Strawberries
- Apples
- Plums
- Beans

By including more of these ingredients in your diet, you are providing yourself with more antioxidants, vitamins, and minerals that will keep your body going strong. They are also beneficial to your mind because they help you focus and think clearly.

When you eat junk food, you feel instant gratification because it tastes good. But because this type of food is not nutritious, you almost always experience some sort of crash after you eat it. This can be subtle, but it often tanks your energy levels, which can put you in an even worse mood.

You can treat yourself to your comfort foods sometimes, but make sure that a majority of your diet consists of whole foods and natural ingredients. These are going to feel especially rejuvenating to you right now. Over time, your body will begin to crave these foods instead of junk food. The more that you stop giving in to your cravings, the more you are promoting change. This does take self-disciple, but you have what it takes to ensure that you are taking better care of yourself during this time. Without a healthy mind and body, your inner systems will begin to deteriorate. Everything is going to start feeling harder and worse.

Grief can often take your hunger away entirely, but you must also use your self-discipline in this case. Even when you do not feel hungry, you need to make sure that you are keeping up with your basic levels of nourishment. The sadness can often mask the feeling of hunger, but your body is still going to feel it intensely. Over time, you are going to become weaker. Before this starts to happen to you, plan out a couple of your meals, and give yourself regular reminders to eat them. While you might not feel like eating a whole portion, getting something nutritious into your stomach is only going to help you during this time.

Part of grief is exploring your options, and this is exactly what the Wim Hof Method provides you—an option to take. It is something unconventional, but it can end up helping you if you are willing to give it a try.

Most people feel discouraged during grief because it feels like happiness is unattainable. This is what happens when you become stuck in your routines. Even when it is hard, try to become brave enough to branch out.

anger, you will be able to assure yourself that you are on the right path toward healing.

There are many things that you can do for yourself during this time to make the grief feel easier. Whether you want to explore Stoicism, the Wim Hof method, professional help, or other holistic activities, never stop believing in the fact that you will be able to feel okay again. You must be willing to give these a try, though. Even if it is something you have never done before, give it a go to see if it can help you.

With all of your tools in mind, the time to heal is now. Do not spend another moment suffering because of your loss. You can turn this time into one of transformation and growth. Use all of the resources you can, and follow your instincts. They will guide you through a lot of the pain and discomfort that arises.

If you enjoy what you have learned from this book, do not forget to leave a review. Tell others about your story and how much you have overcome so far. You can also read about other experiences that people have been through with their grief and trauma. Through inspiration from others, you will be able to gather even more strength to get you through this difficult time.

Feel free to add me on Instagram (@cortezranieri) and send me a DM with your story and how this book may have helped. If you haven't already, check out my first book, *10 Habits For Grief and Loss*. Thank you so much for taking the time to read this book, it means the world to me!

REFERENCES

10 Simple Ways to Improve Your Self-Awareness [With Examples]. *Nick Wignall.* (2020, October 29). https://nickwignall.com/self-awareness/.

The Benefits of Breathing Exercises: Wim Hof Method. The Benefits of Breathing Exercises | *Wim Hof Method.* https://www.wimhofmethod.com/breathing-exercises.

Cherry, K. (2019, July 17). How Attachment Theory Works. *Verywell Mind.* https://www.verywellmind.com/what-is-attachment-theory-2795337.

Cherry, K. (2020, March 29). How John Bowlby Influenced Child Psychology. *Verywell Mind.* https://www.verywellmind.com/john-bowlby-biography-1907-1990-2795514.

Crowther, L. (2020, July 30). The Five Stages of Grief and Loss. *Legacy.com*. https://www.legacy.com/advice/the-five-stages-of-grief/.

Dudley, D. (2020, March 29). Seneca. *Encyclopædia Britannica*. https://www.britannica.com/biography/Lucius-Annaeus-Seneca-Roman-philosopher-and-statesman.

Elisabeth Kübler-Ross Biography. *EKR Foundation*. https://www.ekrfoundation.org/elisabeth-kubler-ross/biography/.

Franks, D. (2015, May 26). Understanding: Knowing the Connection Between Anger and Grief. *Crossroads Hospice Charitable Foundation*. https://crhcf.org/insights/understanding-the-anger-caused-by-grief/.

Frazer Consultants. (2020, August 17). Grief Theories Series: Parkes and Bowlby's Four Phases of Grief. *Frazer Consultants*. https://frazerconsultants.com/2018/03/grief-theories-series-parkes-and-bowlbys-four-phases-of-grief/.

Gill, N. (2019, October 25). Does the Serenity Prayer Echo the Greco-Roman Notion of Stoicism? *ThoughtCo*. https://www.thoughtco.com/stoics-and-moral-philosophy-4068536.

Hairston, S. (2019, July 11). How Grief Shows Up In Your Body. *WebMD*. https://www.webmd.com/special-reports/grief-stages/20190711/how-grief-affects-your-body-and-mind.

Holland, K. (2019, January 29). How to Control Anger: 25 Tips to Manage Your Anger and Feel Calmer. *Healthline*. https://www.healthline.com/health/mental-health/how-to-control-anger.

How to Deal With Depression: Wim Hof Method. How to Deal With Depression | *Wim Hof Method*. https://www.wimhofmethod.com/how-to-deal-with-depression.

Jewell, T. (2017, December 8). Depression vs. Complicated Grief. *Healthline.* https://www.healthline.com/health/depression/complicated-grief.

Kashdan, T., & Biswas-Diener, R. (2014, October 20). The Right Way to Get Angry. *Greater Good.* https://greatergood.berkeley.edu/article/item/the_right_way_to_get_angry.

Mayo Clinic. (2016, October 19). What is grief? https://www.mayoclinic.org/patient-visitor-guide/support-groups/what-is-grief.

Nesbitt, A. (2020, October 24). Khabib Nurmagomedov collapsed in tears after beating Justin Gaethje at UFC 254. *USA Today.* https://ftw.usatoday.com/2020/10/ufc-254-khabib-nurmagomedov-cries-after-beating-justin-gaethje.

Perper, R. (2019, July 2). Are You Avoiding Your Grief? *Therapy Changes.* https://therapychanges.com/blog/2018/03/avoiding-grief/.

Popova, M. (2018, November 13). Epictetus on Love and Loss: The Stoic Strategy for Surviving Heartbreak. *Brain Pickings.* https://www.brainpickings.org/2018/08/26/epictetus-love-loss/.

Popova, M. (2018, November 13). Marcus Aurelius on Mortality and the Key to Living Fully. *Brain Pickings.* https://www.brainpickings.org/2015/11/18/marcus-aurelius-meditations-mortality/.

Popova, M. (2018, November 13). Seneca on Grief and the Key to Resilience in the Face of Loss: An Extraordinary Letter to His Mother. *Brain Pickings*. https://www.brainpickings.org/2017/05/02/seneca-consolation-to-helvia/.

Pritchard, E. (2018, July 17). 20 physical, behavioural and emotional symptoms of bereavement and how to overcome them. *Country Living*. https://www.countryliving.com/uk/wellbeing/a21549981/physical-emotional-behavioural-symptoms-grief-bereavement-how-overcome/.

Romm, C. (2014, September 11). Understanding How Grief Weakens the Body. *The Atlantic*. https://www.theatlantic.com/health/archive/2014/09/understanding-how-grief-weakens-the-body/380006/.

Ropchan, J. (2013, March 14). 5 Common Grief Avoidance Patterns - *Your Tribute*. http://resources.yourtribute.com/grief-and-loss/grief-avoidance-patterns/.

Schwartz, A. The Difference Between Grief and Depression, The DSM V. *Mental Help*. https://www.mentalhelp.net/blogs/the-difference-between-grief-and-depression-the-dsm-v/.

The Science Behind The Wim Hof Method | *Wim Hof Method*. https://www.wimhofmethod.com/science.

Shermer, M. (2008, November 1). Five Fallacies of Grief: Debunking Psychological Stages. *Scientific American*. https://www.scientificamerican.com/article/five-fallacies-of-grief/.

Sinicki, A. (2018, November 5). Explaining the Wim Hof Method. *The Bioneer*. https://www.thebioneer.com/explaining-wim-hof-method/.

A Stoic Response to Grief. *Daily Stoic*. (2017, September 25). https://dailystoic.com/stoic-response-grief/.

Stoicism And Depression Teach A Valuable Lesson About Lockdown Grief. *MindThatEgo*. (2020, June 2). https://www.mindthatego.com/negative-visualisation/.

UHC Newsroom. (2020, June 17). Anxiety-Fighting Foods that May Help Bring Calm, Balance. *Newsroom*. https://newsroom.uhc.com/health/anti-anxiety.html?Source=Google.

What Is Stoicism? A Definition & 9 Stoic Exercises To Get You Started. *Daily Stoic*. (2020, May 8). https://dailystoic.com/what-is-stoicism-a-definition-3-stoic-exercises-to-get-you-started/.

Who Is Epictetus? From Slave To World's Most Sought After Philosopher. *Daily Stoic*. (2020, August 31). https://dailystoic.com/epictetus/.

Who Is Marcus Aurelius? Getting To Know The Roman Emperor. *Daily Stoic*. (2020, August 31). https://dailystoic.com/marcus-aurelius/.

Who Is Seneca? Inside The Mind of The World's Most Interesting Stoic. *Daily Stoic*. (2020, August 19). https://dailystoic.com/seneca/.

Wikimedia Foundation. (2020, October 21). Five stages of grief. *Wikipedia*. https://en.wikipedia.org/wiki/Five_stages_of_grief.

Wolfelt, A. (2018, October 17). Grieving vs. Mourning: *TAPS. taps tragedy assistance program survivors.* https://www.taps.org/articles/24-3/grieving-vs-mourning.